Fairfield
At Creation

Fairfield
At Creation

Robert F. Wessel

Writers Club Press
San Jose New York Lincoln Shanghai

Fairfield At Creation

Writers Club Press
an imprint of iUniverse, Inc.

For information address:
iUniverse, Inc.
5220 S. 16th St., Suite 200
Lincoln, NE 68512
www.iuniverse.com

ISBN: 0-595-22293-5

Printed in the United States of America

To My Wife, Helen

Without whose persistent encouragement this tale would never have been told.

R.F.W.

Finagle's Rule No. 6: Do not believe in miracles—rely on them.

CONTENTS

FOREWORD

This recollection of the events and conditions existing in 1953, as they pertain to the formation of the Village and City of Fairfield, Ohio, was begun about 20 years ago. I toyed with it off and on since that time, but lacked the necessary impetus to complete it until now.

As I reviewed my notes, it has eerily dawned on me that of all of persons I refer to in my chronicle, Grace Hoelle and I are the only survivors.

I am the sole survivor of the elected council and officers and the only Village of Fairfield slate.

Grace and I are the only survivors of the first elected council and officers of the City of Fairfield, Ohio.

My goal is an impossible one. I want to recreate the feelings, concerns and ambience that existed from 1953 forward. I want to reflect, and I hope you will, too, on the major events that have brought our City to its present respected niche.

Robert F. Wessel
August 8, 2001

ACKNOWLEDGEMENTS

I wish to acknowledge with deep appreciation Tarana Ervin, my secretary and fellow author. Her skills, advice and encouragement were invaluable in the completion of this book.

R.F.W.

CHAPTER I

The Background

The story of Fairfield is of a village that could not be formed, but was, and of a city that could not succeed, but has.

Since this chronicle will reflect the events leading up to the formation of the Village of Fairfield, and continuing through the first two years that Fairfield was a city, it is appropriate that you know something of my background. This should help you to assess the events with the proper frame of reference and, if you observed or participated in this span of Fairfield history, to understand why there was not always a concert of opinion on every Fairfield event.

Fairfield was conceived in the year 1953 A.D. At that time, I had been a resident of the community all of two years. My wife, Helen, and I had been married for two years and our major concern was to complete our dream house and live in suburban bliss ever after.

Helen and I were both born and raised in the City of Hamilton. Helen graduated from old Hamilton High and Miami University. I attended Hamilton schools until I had completed my sophomore year in high school, when my family moved to Oxford, Ohio, and I entered and graduated from Oxford Stewart High School. I completed two years at Miami University.

It was now October, 1942. World War II was gaining momentum and I was called into service in the Army of the United States. I served for 38 months with the 908th Field Artillery Battalion of the 83rd Infantry Division. We were dispatched to the European Theater of Operations in

April, 1944. Our Division participated in all five of the European campaigns. I returned to the United States in December, 1945, and was discharged from service.

The war ended and it was time to think of career. After some false sputterings and a general sense of aimlessness, I completed my legal training at Salmon P. Chase School of Law. I must say at this point that I really owe my legal career to two people: My mother, whose determination kept me in school; and, my wife, Helen, who gave me the incentive to be a lawyer by her firm belief that I had the potential and ability to serve my community as a capable lawyer.

While I was completing my legal studies, I had several full time jobs since Salmon P. Chase was a night law school. I was employed by the State of Ohio, Bureau of Employment Services for one and a half years, and as Personnel Director for Columbia Machinery and Engineering Company for two years. I passed the Ohio State Bar examination in June 1951, and was married two days later. I was sworn in as a lawyer in October 1951 by the Chief Justice of the Ohio Supreme Court and began to practice as a Butler County lawyer shortly thereafter. When the Fairfield issue began, I had a total of one and one-half years practice before the Bar, and I was just beginning to understand the complexities of being a lawyer in private practice.

My first glimmer that all was not right in Fairfield suburbia came in mid-summer of 1953. Gilbert E. "Gus" Condo and Carl M. Kollstedt, brother lawyers and each a life-long resident of Fairfield Township, asked me to attend a meeting to be held in the Fairfield High School. Together, they made a very preliminary study of incorporating a part of the township as a village, and the purpose of the meeting was to enable them to report to the informal group exploring the question and to also hear from Jackson Bosch, then Butler County Prosecuting Attorney, on the question of taxes, evaluation and costs of incorporating.

The meeting was held in July 1953, on a hot, sultry Sunday afternoon as only the Ohio Valley can produce. "Meeting" is a generic term that encompasses just about every social and business occasion when humans get together. To most of those assembled on this summer Sunday afternoon, it was a gathering of long time acquaintances for the purpose of solving a community problem. To me, it was a time of assessment. What is the problem? Who are the people?

The problem was simple to understand. Did the southward expansion of the City of Hamilton represent a threat to the continued existence of the Fairfield School District? If so, is incorporation as a village the solution?

To the Fairfieldians assembled, there was little question that the southward expansion of the City of Hamilton was a real and eminent threat. It was time to circle the wagons. This threat to the core of Fairfield life must be resisted with full commitment and total dedication. The meeting began with a brief explanation of what the procedure would be to incorporate all or part of the township into a village. Gus Condo handled this task with ease, and the group seemed to relax, apparently thinking each to himself that we could certainly handle that problem.

The villain of the meeting, in the person of Jackson Bosch, Butler County Prosecutor, was the next speaker. A more unlikely villain has rarely been seen here or elsewhere. Jack was a congenial, witty, top-notch lawyer. He was well-liked by bench and bar. For him to appear at a Sunday afternoon meeting seemed to me above and beyond the call of duty. He began by explaining the many duties and services that are required of village government. He explained about police protection, fire protection, street maintenance and repair. He touched on sewers, water and garbage collection. He hinted at zoning and planning. So far, so good. We who were giving his every word our undivided attention nodded in agreement. We could certainly solve those problems.

Then came the kicker: To do all of these extraordinary things that every village and city, large and small, is required to do takes a great deal of money. The question was, from where was this vast sum of money going to come?

There are two general questions on which the average American is blissfully ignorant. One of these is the internal working of the human body. The other is how tax money is spent. The natural assumption is that when we pay our taxes twice yearly, that all of that money comes right back to our community, and can be used by local government for any lawful community purpose. This assumption was the general feeling of most of those assembled on this hot, sultry Sunday afternoon, me included. "Professor" Bosch was about to begin Lesson One.

We soon learned that citizens united in common purpose and commitment cannot ignore those commitments which other citizens united in other common purposes have previously made. Jack succinctly pointed out a few of those previous commitments. He told us about funding our school system, and that over half of all taxes collected were directed to paying the cost. He told us about paying for County government and the tax money it costs. He told us about bonded indebtedness, special tax levies, State government, and Fairfield Township costs. We didn't understand the details, but we got the message: *Incorporation was going to raise taxes.*

Professor Bosch, with the instinct of a good trial lawyer, could sense that it was time for the "kill". If Jack had any failing, indeed if it even were a failing, it was that he couldn't distinguish between kill and overkill. With the hyperbole common to all prosecutors, he began to paint a word picture of costs, taxes, bureaucratic red tape and hardship that fairly boggled the mind. By the time that he had finished his summation, a glassy-eyed group of Fairfield citizens could tell you that the only thing more difficult to bear than a hot, sultry, humid Sunday in the Miami Valley, is a hot, sultry, humid Sunday on which a pall has descended.

The meeting didn't last much longer. It wasn't from any diminishment of purpose, but rather from a sense of confusion and indecision. There was no agreement to meet in the future. It was the end of a meeting that required personal reflection on the part of each participant to set the schedule for future events.

That afternoon and evening, I thought about the meeting and my conclusion was that, in the absence of some positive event, incorporation would not occur in Fairfield Township. This conclusion resulted from the fact that I did not fully understand the intensity of the issue, what with being a new Fairfield resident, but with a full understanding that the only desire of those who attended the meeting, as nearly as I could ascertain, was a maintenance of the status quo. I was mistaken on all accounts.

Since I didn't understand the historical significance of the day, I must confess that I cannot reproduce an accurate roster of who were present at this first meeting. I know that Bosch, Kollstedt, Condo and I were there. I remember Walter Hunter, Winifred C. Field, Grace Hoelle, Warren Harding, Warren Steele, and Martha Seward Rahfuse. Of the latter group, the only person I had previously met was Warren Harding, and I certainly didn't know that in the succeeding years, we would all be working toward a common goal.

Since the history of Fairfield is, essentially, a story of people and how they shaped events, understanding the narrative would probably be enhanced if you meet some them, particularly if you see them as I saw them; ready to embark on this great adventure.

Twice in my lifetime thus far have I had the wonderful experience of working and associating with completely dedicated and totally committed American citizens. The first was during my service with the 908th Field Artillery battalion, 83rd Infantry Division during World War II. The second was working with the people you are about to meet in the formation and establishment of the Village and City of Fairfield.

First, the Fairfield Pioneers, present at both conception and birth:

Gilbert E. "Gus" Condo. A lifelong resident of Fairfield Township, and fully experienced trial lawyer, known and respected throughout Butler County. He brought to the project the one indispensible quality that it must have to succeed—credibility. It is ironic that when incorporation of the entire township failed, it took Gus out of the mainstream of corporate activity, but he was in the battle from start to incorporation. He has never been recognized as he should have been.

Carl M. Kollstedt. In the melee from the start, "Coke" was a legal research-oriented lawyer who frequently came up with an obscure and archaic case that saved the day. Born and raised in Fairfield, known to all Township officials, he was an indispensable cog in the politics of the situation. First Fairfield Solicitor and first Fairfield Municipal Judge.

Winifred C. Field. The rock of the Fairfield incorporation. She was the conscience of the community. She was quietly vocal in guiding the affairs of the committee for incorporation. Her home was the frequent gathering place for those interested in Fairfield. She was totally dedicated to the good of Fairfield. First and longtime Treasurer of the Village and City of Fairfield, she and I had many a battle, many a disagreement, and through it all, remained close friends. She represented those qualities that make Fairfield great.

Walter L. Hunter. Explosive Father of the Fairfield Waterworks, it was his petition which led to the formation of the Village of Fairfield. Dedicated to the proposition that no one outside of Fairfield Township could tell Fairfieldians who was going to govern them. If you were within a mile's range of Walt, you knew his opinion on any subject that had been or was being discussed. Served on the first Village and City Council. An able legislator attuned to the needs of the electorate. Great companion.

Kenneth L. Faist, Jr. Quiet, competent and a silent force in the formation of the Village of Fairfield. When there was a tough assignment, such as getting the word out about meetings, voting or general information, Ken was the one we turned to. He and his father, Kenneth L. Faist, had earned the respect of many Fairfield residents. Their support induced many voters to support incorporation. Valued member of the only Village Council.

Warren L. Harding. Pillar of the Fairfield Grange, longtime Director of the Butler County Welfare Department, champion of the Fairfield School System. From the start, he was an avid supporter of Fairfield incorporation and, until his death, he continued his interest in every question that concerns the quality of life in the city. He was a tireless researcher of information vital to Fairfield voters considering the question of incorporation.

Warren L. Steele. A tireless worker for the incorporation. He was the leader of many Fairfieldians who looked to and followed his leadership. On the majority of questions that arose in the course of reaching city status, he and I were in almost total disagreement. As the years passed, we developed a grudging respect for one another that reached the point of casual friendship. This is not to denigrate the contributions that he made to the incorporation, which were valuable and continuing. He was one of my opponents for the office of Village Mayor and later served as a City Councilman.

Next, two ladies, like Benedictine and Brandy, need to be classified together. They worked as a team from the first meeting of interested Fairfieldians until city status was obtained. They were cheerleaders of the movement, and tireless do-ers of what needed to be done. They are:

Marguerite Burkett. A good writer, she composed and edited many of the newsletters that were delivered to all Fairfield voters. She had a sparkling personality, and was an inspiration to the group, particularly when the situation and outlook was gloomy. She was available for any needed Fairfield task. She was the editor of the *Fairfield Chronicle* during 1957. She made the November election of that year very interesting.

Carrie Burnett. A Stockton resident and close friend of Marguerite Burkett. The two worked as a team, and performed every task needed to achieve a successful Fairfield incorporation.

Dr. Arthur Schalk. Long-time Fairfield resident, retired Professor of Veterinary Medicine at Ohio State University. Famous for having placed a window in the side of a cow so his students could observe the digestive process. Long-time president of the Fairfield Residents Association, which was the backbone of Fairfield Village and City for many years. He was a force in the development of Fairfield.

John Slade. Member of a pioneer Fairfield family. Big man at WMOH. Great publicist and totally dedicated to the incorporation of Fairfield.

Helen B. Wessel. My wife. A dedicated, active and purposeful advocate of the incorporation of Fairfield from the start.

Joseph and Grace Hoelle. Pioneers in every sense of the word. Critical participants in the Stockton annexation.

Members of the Fairfield Residents Association. This Association was formed in 1954. Walter Hunter was the first chairman. Dr. Arthur Schalk was his successor. The roster of members contains many persons who became prominent in early Fairfield affairs, and probably some of them should be included in the list of Founders. The Association continued as the force in our City through the 1980-1990 decade. It was the sponsor of many historic Village and City events.

Nonetheless, all of us had settled into a summer stupor, and had shelved the idea of incorporation. It was a short surcease.

CHAPTER II

The Explosion

On Thursday, August 6, 1953, the *Hamilton-Journal and Daily News* carried the following headline: *"Council Approves Proposed Annexation."* It refers to a column headed, *"City to Annex Six Districts Under Plan."*

One of the areas to be annexed was in southeast Fairfield Township. The southeast corner would be at the intersection of Gilmore Road and Route 4 (Dixie Highway), and the southwest corner would be at Fairfield where the River Road turns at right angles to the south.

The body of the article stated:

> *"The annexation plan proposes that an area extending about one mile out from the present corporation limits of the city be annexed during a period of several years. The area is broken down into six districts, each controlled by populated plats so that they could be handled individually by petitions…".*

> *"…6—The area of the southeast of the city in Fairfield Township to a point beyond Gilmore and Nilles Rds."**

The proposed area included the Fairfield High School, Fisher Body Plant and all other industry and manufacturing businesses located in Fairfield Township.

The ink on *Hamilton Journal-News* of August 3, 1953, was not yet dry when those Fairfieldians who had been investigating incorporation called an emergency meeting to devise a plan that would save our community and preserve our way of life.

Only a few minutes of the meeting were spent in determining what could be done. It was painfully obvious that our only hope was to incorporate enough of the territory to preclude annexation by the City of Hamilton. That decided, the next three hours of the meeting were spent in deciding what part of Fairfield Township should be included.

Those people who were in attendance at the meeting were a true cross-section of Fairfield Township. During the course of the evening, many plans were advanced, but each of them had one drawback—they omitted a part of the Township where someone in attendance lived.

As the evening dragged on, it became apparent that there was only one solution:

Incorporate the entire township.

This decision provoked a thunderous burst of applause and, when it had died down, left Messers. Condo, Kollstedt and Wessel with a perplexing question:

How do you incorporate the entire Township?

(*All bold and italicized writing reflects newspaper accounts of events.)

The meeting was adjourned for one week, with the understanding that at the next meeting, the incorporation petitions would be in the hands of the committee and incorporation would be off and running.

Condo, Kollstedt and I agreed that we would meet the next day to begin working on a plan for incorporation.

It wasn't as though we were totally ignorant of the law on the subject of incorporation. We knew that a petition for incorporation could be presented either to the Board of County Commissioners or to the Fairfield Township Trustees. We knew what qualifications the petitioner-signers were required to have. We knew the time frame for presentation of the petitions, who had to be notified, what matters of evidence we had to present to the Board or Trustees. We knew about the voters in the area of incorporation having the right to approve or disapprove the plan. The question was whether the Board of Commissioners or the Township Trustees were more likely to approve the plan that was a prerequisite to any vote of the electorate.

It was a true dilemma since the Board of County Commissioners has to run countywide and, therefore, would count heavily on the voters of Hamilton, the county seat as well as the largest block of votes, on the one hand, as opposed to the Township Trustees, who would be asked to approve an incorporation which, if successful, would result in these Township Trustees seeing their offices eliminated.

The problem was resolved rather quickly since we felt we had no chance of success before the County Commissioners, who we felt would act in whatever fashion was in the best interest for the City of Hamilton.

That is, two-thirds of the Commission would. One of the members of the Commission was Arthur Reiff, a long-time Fairfield Township resident, dedicated to retaining the political integrity of the Fairfield Township area. The other two members of the Commission were Ben Van Gordan and Gordon Augsperger, whom we felt were not enthralled with the idea of another municipal corporation in the county.

The Fairfield Township Trustees were decidedly our best bet. Their collective philosophy was *better a Fairfield incorporation than no Fairfield at all.* George Schierling, who was Clerk of the Fairfield Township Trustees, was a particular advocate of Fairfield incorporation.

The petition to incorporate the entire township was duly prepared. It was circulated, signed by resident freeholders sufficient in number so that it could be filed with the Board of Fairfield Township Trustees on December 17, 1953.

CHAPTER III

The Battle For Incorporation

The road to Fairfield incorporation was a rocky one. It was strewn with obstacles and impediments.

While our group was diligently seeking valid signatures on our petitions for incorporation, there were other Fairfield Township groups doing exactly the same thing, seeking signatures for incorporating only a part of the township.

Getting the signatures required informing the signers of the advantages to incorporation. We conducted many meetings throughout the Township extolling the benefits of incorporation, and negating the concerns of those who questioned the financial consequences of incorporation.

We were not alone. The other groups were doing the same thing. It became a race to see which group could get its petition filed first.

The crux of the situation was who was going to have the industry within its boundaries. Fisher Body was the key, and as Fisher Body went, so went Fairfield School. All parties who were orating on the subject were really speaking from the abysmal depths of ignorance. Some thought that every penny in taxes collected from the people who lived in the incorporated area would go to the new village. Actually, only $1.00 of taxes for each $1,000.00 of evaluation was available.

The other side of the coin was the concern of many that taxes would be raised to astronomical levels by the new village to provide services and to pay the expenses of village administration. The proposed budgets showing tax receipts on the one hand and projected village expenses on the other, seem quaint when now examined, but were deadly serious business as the discussion of incorporation gathered momentum.

Completing and executing a petition for incorporation is a difficult and arduous project. The language of the petition must be precise. The numerous requirements of Ohio statutes on this subject must be met. The signers must be resident freeholders. To succeed becomes a time-consuming project.

Warren Steele was the agent for the petitioners on our Petition for Incorporation. Thus, it became known as the "Steele Petition".

Oakley Wooten was the agent for the petitioners for one of the other groups. He was a long term Clerk of the Board of Township Trustees. Thus, it became known as the "Wooten Petition".

Walter Morton was the agent for the third group of aspiring incorporators. Thus, it became known as the "Morton Petition".

The petitions were filed with the Clerk of the Board of Township Trustees in the following order:

December 16, 1953	Petition to incorporate part of Fairfield Township (Wooten) filed with Clerk
December 17, 1953	Petition to incorporate entire Township of Fairfield (Steele) filed with Clerk
February 27, 1954	Petition for incorporation of South Fairfield, a part of Fairfield Township (Morton) filed with the Clerk.

The Board of Trustees set the Wooten Petition and the Steele Petition for hearing on April 3, 1954.

The Wooten Petition was the first filed and, on its face, was a valid petition. But it failed one critical test that was required of incorporation proceedings in 1954. It was unreasonable in size and shape. Most of the territory was in the northeastern quadrant of Fairfield Township with a neck extending south and west to include General Motors, American Cyanamide and the Fairfield Central Schools.

Oakley Wooten was a long term Clerk of the Fairfield Board of Township Trustees, so that it stood to reason that he would have the ears of the Trustees. It didn't work out that way, which says a great deal about the men who held these positions.

The Warren Steele Petition, which was sponsored by our groups, remains very fresh in my mind. Logically, since it encompassed the entire township, it seemed the method most likely to maintain the status quo. To the Fairfield Residents Association, our group, it was eminently reasonable. The Fairfield Residents Association was a totally dedicated group. Its creed was *"Keep Fairfield, Fairfield."* We were borderline fanatics. We didn't realize that there were people, good people, who didn't want Fairfield incorporated.

After about two hours of hearing, the Board of Township Trustees rejected the Wooten Petition; accepted the Steele Petition, and ordered an election on the question: *Should the area be incorporated?* to be held on April 17, 1954?

This caused an intensive publicity campaign to be waged by the Fairfield Residents Association for the incorporation. Since, at that time, the only newspaper was the *Hamilton Journal-News,* a publication definitely not in favor of the incorporation, the main thrust of the campaign was mimeographed flyers stuffed in the mailboxes of prospective voters. If you don't remember, let it be said that the voters who got the last faint 20 copies had to call the sender to interpret what was printed. WMOH radio made a timely announcement of the date of the election, but took no stand on the issue.

The Wooten petitioners filed an action *in mandamus* to compel the Board of Fairfield Township Trustees to accept their petition. This matter was heard before Judge P.P. Boli on April 13, 1954, whereupon their petition for a writ was denied.

The election on the question of incorporation for all of Fairfield was held on April 17, 1954, and incorporation was rejected by the voters. The results were:

> For incorporation   831
>
> Against incorporation   1,219

Fairfield Township, as of 1954, was essentially an agricultural community. At least 85% of the area was farmland. Farmers believed that farms didn't belong in villages or cities. Farmers vote. Fairfield farmers voted against incorporation.

Besides this, there were essentially two factions in Fairfield Township. The people who lived on the "Knob", which is sort of a euphemism for that part of the township that lies north of Bobmeyer Road, east of the old Pennsylvania RR, south of State Route 4 as it meanders from Hamilton toward Middletown, and east of the Route 4 Bypass. They had a natural interest in establishing an organized community where it had long been resisted.

The other faction was our group, the Fairfield Residents Association, which we didn't believe, then or now, was a faction, but rather were the true keepers of the faith.

There was a sizeable group that just didn't want anything to happen.

While the effort to incorporate the entire township was at fever pitch, some of the group—Walter Hunter, Gus Condo, Carl Kollstedt and I—thought we should have a back-up plan just in case the entire township incorporation plan didn't succeed.

We selected that area of Fairfield Township where incorporation would likely succeed and proposed a petition to incorporate it. This area shows on the sketch below:

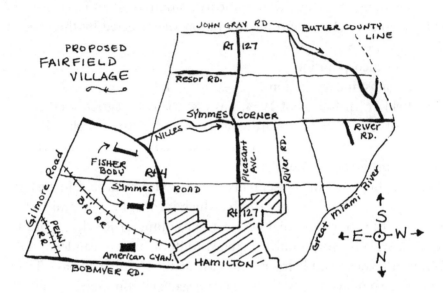

A petition to incorporate with necessary proofs as to this area of Fairfield Township was filed April 14, 1954, with the Fairfield Township clerk. Walter Hunter was the agent for the incorporation and, thus, the petition was known as the "Hunter Petition".

This was a fortuitous happening, but it did face a vexing obstacle. There was yet pending with the Fairfield Board of Township Trustees the Morton Petition, which had been filed on February 27, 1954. It was held in abeyance while the petition to incorporate the entire township was processed. Although the petition was filed on February 27, 1954, the necessary proofs as to electors was not filed until April 16, 1954.

On June 5, 1954, a petition carrying 84 signatures of the original 107 signers of the Morton Petition was filed with the Township Trustees asking that their names be withdrawn from the Morton Petition.

On June 25, 1954, nineteen of the original signers who had signed a petition to withdraw their names, filed a petition with the Township Trustees asking that their names be reinstated on the original petition.

At the hearing on June 25, 1954, the Township Trustees considered the Morton Petition, and deferred a decision until they could confer with their advisor, Prosecutor Jackson Bosch.

They also considered the Hunter Petition, but made no decision pending the decision on Morton.

After conferring with Mr. Bosch at a special meeting on June 28, 1954, the Trustees rejected the Morton Petition, and approved the Hunter Petition. They ordered an election on the question to be held on Saturday, July 10, 1954.

Another period of frenetic activity ensued. Public meetings, daily articles in the *Journal-News.*

On July 8th, the lead editorial was entitled: *"Serious Decisions in Fairfield"*

> *"Voters in an area of Fairfield Township south of Hamilton, will decide, at a special election Saturday, whether or not that area will be incorporated as a village.*
>
> *The importance of this decision should not be over-looked. It carries many and varied responsibilities. It can, without doubt, be the stepping stone to incorporation of a city instead of a village if and when the area has a population of 5,000. That automatically brings a city status and city responsibilities.*
>
> *Responsibilities are many, whether in a village or city. And the people of Fairfield Township will, we hope, carry these responsibilities seriously as they go to the polls Saturday. They are writing their own tickets for the future.*

Two of the heavy responsibilities, as we see them, are water and sewers. As said before, no area even moderately populated can long exist with individual septic tanks and wells. The two, in small areas, just do not go together for the health of the community.

Therefore, the two services needed most are water and sewers—a water system and a sewage system with a sewage disposal plant.

Water supply, unless a community is on a large stream, is, as everyone knows, an uncertainty. Underground water can be a certainty only when it is found and thoroughly tested. Wells can go dry and be damaged quickly, often without apparent reason.

Sewers and sewage disposal are tremendous problems—and extremely expensive, not just in construction but in upkeep.

And, as said many times before, there are no such things as bargains in taxation. People get what they pay for and pay for what they get, regardless of what may have been the theme songs of many politicians down through the ages."

And, on July 9th, under the heading, *"Fairfield's Future"*, they opined:

"The decision is up to the people themselves and the hope therefore is that registered voters in the area take advantage of their right to vote and help make the important decision Saturday.

There is also, on this eve of the vote, a most sincere hope that the people residing in this area of Fairfield

Township understand the seriousness of the proposal before them—understand the obligations and responsibilities that go with incorporation.

It is hoped that residents of the area recognize the responsibilities and the cost of services, like water and sewage, the problems of zoning and protecting the value of their properties. These are serious problems confronting every owner of property.

To believe that persons can live more cheaply one place than another if they receive the same service is a mistake made by many. To believe that there are any bargains or cut rates in taxation for public service is accepting only the prediction of a politician or office-seeker. To believe, as already indicated by inquiries made in the area about the cost of water plants, that water and sewage are not immediate problems, is to ignore the facts."

In the meantime, the supporters of the Morton Petition had filed suit in Butler County Common Pleas Court seeking a *writ of mandamus*, ordering the Fairfield Board of Township Trustees to accept the Morton Petition. The matter was set before Fred B. Cramer on Monday, July 5, 1954. After a half-day hearing, Judge Cramer denied the writ. His decision was appealed to the 1st District Court of Appeals and, eventually, rejected by that Court.

The voters in the area, seeking incorporation, went to the polls on Saturday, July 10th. The results of the election were:

For incorporation	738
Against incorporation	216

On July 22nd, the Board of Township Trustees met and certified the results to the Butler County Recorder and, ten days later, the certification was forwarded to the Secretary of the State of Ohio, and Fairfield was officially a Village.

This synopsis of events cannot convey the high pitch of emotions extant during all of the foregoing proceedings. Nor can it record the seemingly unlimited number of meetings, court hearings, and documents filed by *Messers.* Condo, Kollstedt and Wessel during this highly contentious period of local history.

CHAPTER IV

Early Village Days

After the flush of becoming a village had subsided, the question became who would serve as officers. How did I happen to become a candidate for Mayor? It should be an easy question to answer but, in retrospect, it isn't as simple as I thought.

Certain people seemed earmarked for certain jobs. It was pretty obvious to me that Winifred Field was going to be Treasurer of the Village. It just followed as night does day. It was just as obvious that Carl Kollstedt wanted to be Village Solicitor. There was no serious question about this for any number of reasons. He was a lifelong Fairfield resident, had been active in the incorporation of Fairfield from its inception, and was well-known in the community. The Solicitor was appointed, not elected. The position was his.

Following our victory at the polls when the Village of Fairfield became reality, Condo, Kollstedt and I had several meetings to discuss the many legal matters which followed in the wake of the election, and I recall that we discussed on some of these occasions who the Village officers were likely to be, and what effect this would have on the future of the Village. At one of these meetings, the suggestion was made that I seek the office of Mayor.

At that moment, I really didn't give the matter very serious consideration. When I arrived home, I did mention the matter to Helen. We discussed the matter in some detail over the next few days, and she pointed out that the Village was going to need all of the legal help it could get in its infancy, and that my legal training was one talent I possessed to the exclusion of all of the other likely candidates. We were both very interested in making the Village a success. Our discussions enlarged on the subject over the next few days, at which point we decided I should be a candidate for Mayor of the Village of Fairfield.

One of the most fascinating periods of our lives was about to begin.

The question was: *How do you get elected?*

The very newness of the Village provided a textbook demonstration of non-partisan politics in operation. Everyone was an independent candidate in the truest sense of the word. While Fairfield was the subject of the hour if you lived here, in the scheme of partisan politics, it was at this moment an event of little significance. The objective was to garner enough votes to be elected by your own efforts.

Running for political office was a pristine experience for each of us, so we set about learning all we could about how to be elected. We first did the obvious acts which politicians from the birth of the Republic have been doing. We had campaign cards printed, we made signs, we composed a letter partly biographical and partly explanatory. Here's what I have been, and here is here we need to go, and here's what I can do to help us get there. Sort of an epistle.

We analyzed our opponents. There were three other candidates for mayor. Warren Steele and William Holden, whom we knew from the committee to incorporate, and William Pennekamp, who we did not know.

Warren Steele had been active in the incorporation movement from its beginning. He had a group of friends who were also active in achieving incorporation. He was a Fairfield resident for many years, was well-known, and seemed to be the most formidable of the other candidates.

William Holden has also been active in the incorporation of the village, but had joined the group at a somewhat later time than Steele and I. He was a lifelong Fairfield resident, and a graduate of Fairfield High School. Many members of his family had been active in Fairfield

Township activities, and he had a block of votes from this group at the start, which I knew would be difficult to overcome.

William Pennekamp was an unknown threat. He and I were definitely dark horse candidates.

We recognized that we needed to take some action to get acquainted with the Fairfield voters. Helen came up with what proved to be a brilliant idea. She suggested that I pick out a neighborhood each evening and Saturday that I could spare, and go door-to-door to meet the voters. Beginning in late August and continuing right up to election, I spent my spare time in the neighborhoods of Fairfield. It was a challenge, a rewarding one.

On most visits, it was a matter of "*Good Evening. I'm Bob Wessel, a candidate for mayor in November. I'm a lawyer. I've been active in incorporating Fairfield, and I'd like to continue to work at keeping it a good place to live. I would appreciate your support in November.*" Many times there would be questions, usually about taxes or services that let me know just what the concerns and interests of the voters were.

Along the way, I met several candidates for council whom I had not previously known, and I made some new friends. Don Hooven, Jr. is a prime example. I recall that we began arguing about some of the Fairfield problems on that first visit, and that we continued those arguments for many years thereafter until Don moved to Florida. The arguments stopped then, but our friendship continued.

The campaign was lively and interesting. It's always a time for rumors, speculation and just plain gossip. The goal seemed to be to keep the candidates as tense as possible, probably to see how they would react under pressure. There was no shortage of candidates for most of the other offices. There were three candidates for Treasurer, and seventeen for six council seats. Only George Zimmers, who ran for Village Clerk was unopposed.

On reflection, it seems that the primary concern of the new villagers was: *What will the cost of the new Village be?* quickly followed by: *Can we afford it?* At that moment in time, no one had an accurate answer. As we were soon to discover, the breakdown in taxes from the time they are paid by the taxpayer until they are distributed to the State and its various political subdivisions, is a labyrinthian path capable of being followed by few and fully understood by no one.

In a very quick time, it was election day. It seems when you are running for office, you regard the election day something like Christmas Eve during the day—there is nothing to do but wait. Through pure accident, Helen and I learned that one of the most valuable things that you can do is have a competent, friendly voice at the polling place. Helen worked the polls at the firehouse situated at Pleasant Avenue near the only then existing carryout in Fairfield. It was a cold, blustery day and the big event, as far as Helen was concerned, was making the acquaintance of Robert Hunter, father of Walter Hunter. Helen and he disagreed about almost everything, but became fast friends and spent many more election days campaigning, each for their respective causes. I spent the day in the probably futile occupation of going around to all of the polling places to try to get a sense of how the election was going. To tell you the truth, I learned nothing.

Eventually, polls close. Then begins the long wait. It was 10:00 o'clock, and then 11:00 o'clock, and then midnight, and then the wait was over.

We had won.

When the votes were counted, the result was:

Wessel	563
Holden	426
Steele	407

We spent the balance of the time between learning the results and dawn being euphoric, accepting the congratulations of several other candidates who happened by.

By the day after the election, our thoughts had shifted to Samuel Morse's first words on the telegraph that he had invented: *"What has God wrought?"*

The election was wonderful. I hit the trail to my Hamilton office the next morning to accept the congratulations of my friends and fellow lawyers, and the day seemed extremely rosy. It was one of those days when you wanted to live forever. The joy really lasted for a long time, but I must say it was tempered by the fact that there wasn't any honeymoon. Everyone who was elected took office immediately and, believe me, it was off to the races.

Those elected to offices, other than Mayor, were:

Council:	Walter L. Hunter, Charles N. Vance, Ellis R. Muskopf,
	Kenneth L. Faist, Jr., Ben K. Groh and Dr. Robert Mansfield
Treasurer:	Winifred C. Field
Clerk:	George Zimmers

We lost no time in arranging a swearing-in ceremony, which was conducted at the Fairfield High School on the stage of the auditorium on November 22, 1954. Judge Peter Paul Boli, a longtime Fairfield supporter, did the honors and it was a solemn and happy occasion for us all. Judge Boli predicted a great future for the fledgling Village. Everyone in the audience seemed to be in high spirits, and we were all ready to presume future greatness. The Mayor, on these occasions, is expected to respond to set the stage for the administration.

I said:

> *"On behalf of the Council, the Clerk, the Treasurer, and myself, I hereby*
> *accept the duties of office. I pledge myself to do everything within my power to insure a competent and successful government of the Village of Fairfield. We accept these duties with a full knowledge and deep appreciation of the responsibilities and problems which face the Village.*

I know that you who are electors of the Village have elected a civic-spirited Council who are always mindful of the responsibility of office. We are fortunate to have in the Village of Fairfield citizens dedicated to the establishment and promotion of village welfare.

As officers of our community, we ask your support. We shall strive to retain your confidence. In our efforts to establish our government, we ask your patience. All of us are engaged in a new experience in self-government and, at times, you may feel our progress is slow, but we shall meet each problem sincerely and as quickly as consonant with careful and conscientious government.

With the cooperation of each citizen, Fairfield will be a prosperous and happy community."

In retrospect, this seems a ponderous statement to me, but it was true in every respect. The strides that were taken by this group of municipal officers in the short 14 months of Village existence have not been equaled in the 46 years that have since passed.

All of the newly elected officers met the Monday following the swearing-in ceremony to organize and to try to determine how we would proceed. The first meeting was held at the home of the Mayor, and several things became ever more painfully obvious.

In no particular order, they are:

1.   We had no public place at which to hold council meetings.

2.   We had no established procedure to follow. If one were elected to council in Hamilton or Oxford, for example, not only would there be some veterans of the fray to give leadership and guidance, but there would also be the records of the proceedings of the previous officers to follow and an ordered method of procedure already in place. We had

neither, so we explored the Revised Code of Ohio and devised a schedule of meetings and committees, and then put the plan into operation.

3.   The most critical shortage of all was money. Many thought that all we had to do was to announce our presence to the proper fiscal officer, and a stream of money would begin to flow. Since Carl Kollstedt and I both knew that this would not happen, we had been meeting on a frequent basis with the Butler County Auditor and Treasurer, and they finally came up with a contribution of $5,000.00 that, as I recall, came from the Road and Bridge Fund of Fairfield Township. This really wasn't a blessing since, as an incorporated Village, we were responsible for the maintenance and cleaning of Village streets. The money we received was not restricted. It was General Fund money, and we used it, in part, to purchase the necessary office and Village supplies we needed to begin keeping a record of Village procedures.

We began our pursuit of a place to meet by doing what the Ohio Revised Code provided. We filed a petition with the Probate Court of Butler County, Ohio, asking them to make equitable division of property between the Village of Fairfield and Fairfield Township. This required the giving of notice to the Township Trustees, and entailed about a 3-week wait until we could have the hearing.

In our organizational meeting, we had hired and appointed Carl Kollstedt as Village Solicitor, and he and I spent a good part of each working day trying to solve Fairfield problems. On Saturdays and Sundays, we met with Council and the Treasurer to keep them apprised of what was needed and what was transpiring.

During this same period of time, we were having informal meetings with the City of Hamilton officials, and my recollection is that it was about boundaries and the desire of Hamilton to annex territory from St. Clair Avenue in Hamilton south to Symmes Road so that the Hamilton Board of Education could construct George Washington Junior High School. There were other discussions going on at the same time with them. I recall we asked about Hamilton furnishing water to the Village, and other subjects of mutual concern. The major problem was that people in Hamilton, particularly officialdom, just didn't believe that the Village of Fairfield was for real.

By the end of December 1954, Judge Harry F. Walsh, Probate Judge, had decided the question of the division of property between Fairfield Township and the Village of Fairfield. The City of Fairfield became the owner of the township real property on Pleasant Avenue, which consisted of a firehouse and what had been in by-gone years a township meetinghouse. The meetinghouse consisted of a moderately sized room in the front and a very small room in the rear.

We had a place to meet, but no furniture and no other equipment. Fortunately for me, and for the embryo Village, my father-in-law, Carl Brinker, was a sink top and cabinetmaker. He made and contributed to the Village two Formica-topped tables with pedestal bases, and they served as tables for Council, Mayor's court and every other municipal meeting for at least the next ten years, and I'm not sure that even now they may be serving a municipal purpose in some secluded office somewhere in the city labyrinth.

We cleaned up the meetinghouse, and at long last we were ready to go public with our meetings. When the entire finances of the municipality consist of $5,000.00, there is no problem in dealing with priorities. We established very modest salaries for Council, Mayor, Treasurer, and Village Clerk. None of them started until the New Year and, even then, they were in serious doubt.

We were lucky in many ways to be a Village, since a village is only responsible for the care and cleaning of village streets. State highways in a village are the responsibility of the State, and county highways are the responsibility of the County. It was in the deep of winter and the snow-cleaning season, and the village of Fairfield really needed all the help it could get. We really got good service from both County and State, and since the Township was not overly endowed with snow removal equipment, there wasn't too much difference in snow removal by the village as compared to the township, which is to say that either way there wasn't very much.

One of the very early acts of Fairfield Council was to establish the position of Safety Service Director. As soon as the position was established, it was the feeling of Council that the position should be filled as it would give us a liaison with our citizens, and would be a first step in providing those services to the community which we had extolled to encourage our neighbors to join us in forming a village.

This desire to fill the position of Safety Service Director raised a rather interesting question: *With the funding that we had available, who could we hire?* Since this was the very first true employee of the village to be named, it was essential that the person be one who had not only the abilities to do the job, but also the desire to make the vision of Fairfield a credible one. As I've stated, I was a newcomer to Fairfield in the scheme of things, and I certainly didn't have the wide Fairfield acquaintance to enable me to fill the position. Fortunately, we had on Fairfield Council some members who had been lifelong Fairfield residents, and I could look to them for assistance. Walt Hunter, Ken Faist, Ellis Muskopf and Ben Groh had all grown up in Fairfield, and they were more knowledgeable than any *Who's Who* that I could have consulted. To a man, they recommended Paul Conrad.

I promptly called Paul and arranged a meeting. We seemed to understand one another from the start. Paul was a true Fairfield farmer. He knew farming and all the many problems associated with it. He got things done by doing them himself. It was immediately apparent to me that in Fairfield's position, he would be the ideal man for the job. In addition, since he wasn't going to give up farming, he could almost afford to work for what we could pay. I made the appointment, and thus began one of the most unusual relationships that ever existed between a Mayor and a Safety Service Director in Ohio municipal history. I made many appointments as Fairfield Mayor, but I never made a better appointment in my career.

In short order, we purchased a small dump truck and Paul Conrad became not only Safety Service Director, but the entire maintenance department, including snow removal, of the Village of Fairfield. What was great about Paul during this formative period was the fact that he always knew where we could go to get help. If we had a heavy snow, he knew what farmers would help us clear it. The beauty of it all was that it was all volunteer, free to the Village. I doubt that we would have survived without it.

Concurrently, Winifred Field, our Treasurer, Carl Kollstedt, our Solicitor, and I were trying to formulate a budget. It's hard enough when you know what your income will be. It's even harder if you are in a fight to develop income, and you don't know what your income will be.

What was immediately apparent to Miss Field, Kollstedt and myself was that the Village Council could not impose any type of tax on real or personal property without a vote of the citizens. At that time, and probably at this time, political subdivisions within the state were operating on a legislatively mandated 10 mill limitation, which meant that the total of all taxes levied on real and personal property within the area you lived could not exceed ten mils, that is ten dollars per thousand dollars of evaluation. This meant that all of the taxes currently being collected in the new Village of Fairfield had to be totaled to see what, if anything, was left. We totaled and there wasn't.

By the time the deductions in millage for the State of Ohio, Butler County, Fairfield School System and Fairfield Township were completed, there was no millage left within the ten. This translated to one mill or one dollar per thousand sum that would be made available to the Village by deleting it from the Fairfield Township budget, since the township was no longer responsible for the maintenance or repair of the village streets. The ballpark calculation was that this fund would produce for the Village the sum of $28,000.00 per year.

By the end of January 1955, we had submitted a budget to the County Auditor as we were required by law to do. It estimated that we would have about $40,000.00 to spend in the tax year 1955. This was comprised of the $28,000.00 from the road and bridge fund from Fairfield Township, a generous estimation of what the Village might receive from inheritance taxes of residents who died with sufficient assets so that they were taxed, and other miscellaneous sources of tax income that were small, but vital to our survival.

We had, by this time, also learned another interesting fact of tax life, this being that our budget was based on taxes to be paid by our citizens for the tax year 1955. Unfortunately, the real estate and personal property taxes for 1955 would not be collected until 1956. Thus began a hand-to-mouth year of seeking and usually getting cash advancements from the County Auditor to keep us afloat until tax collections caught up with our financial needs. For all the problems, we got through the year 1955 without any major financial crisis. I do not attribute this to luck, but I do attribute it to astute financial management by our Treasurer, Winifred Field.

The primary concern of Council and other village officers at this point, was to identify and to devise a plan for solving the remaining problems crucial to village survival. After a few meetings, the consensus of Village officialdom was that the following problems demanded immediate attention:

The overriding problem was to prevent annexation of territory by the City of Hamilton on the one hand, and to prevent detachment from the Village of Fairfield by farmers, some of whom felt that incorporation of any kind was not to their respective benefits.

In many ways, all of the other concerns were directly related to this issue. While all of the subservient issues were vital in and of themselves, they depended on fruition to our solving this #1 concern.

The next two problems are of absolutely equal rank. They demanded prompt and proper solution since they would establish the credibility of Fairfield and its worthiness to continue to exist as a municipal corporation in Butler County.

Let's start with the problem that the Village could deal with at once: This was zoning. In this bureaucratic era, it may be difficult to believe but, in January 1955, the stark reality of the situation was that outside of municipal corporations, there was no zoning. If Fairfield were to develop with any sense of orderliness, this critical problem needed to be addressed, and was.

We now live in an age when all governmental projects must begin with a "study". Whether it is Parks, Zoning, Waterworks, Sewer or Traffic, nothing can begin unless some expert from as far away as possible advises the appropriate fathers what needs to be done. Once the study is completed, the fathers then spend a long period of time studying the study and, more often than not, decide the study just doesn't truly reach the question that was propounded. Thereupon, the study is abandoned and the fathers go off on their own venture that, of course, they could and should have done in the first place.

A study was fortunately not a Fairfield option. Since we didn't have the Sunshine Law in effect at this time, all Village officials got together with a map showing the corporation boundaries and began our own study about what zoning would be appropriate for our community. What we did would certainly in this sophisticated age be regarded as rudimentary, but in using our combined not inconsiderable talents, we devised a Zoning Ordinance that, despite several subsequent professional studies, has survived almost intact to this date.

At first glance, it seemed a formidable task and, in the final analysis, it was. But the basics of a plan were so obvious that they almost shouted to be recognized. We were thinking of industrial growth as a method to improve our tax base, so that was the question we first considered. When we looked at the map seeking likely zones for industry, we quickly noted the two railroads that ran from north to south reasonably adjacent to Route 4/Dixie Highway. When we further noted that General Motor's Fisher Body Plant and Cyanimide, our principal industries then extant, were located on these railroads, it wasn't too difficult to pick out the heavy, industrial zone.

We next turned to the light industrial zone, and felt it was logical to place it along the west side of Route 4, since this area did not have access to a rail siding, one of the major distinctions between light and heavy industry.

Commercial zoning seemed reasonable for the properties fronting on our major highways, and we placed commercial zoning on most of the sites along Dixie Highway and Pleasant Avenue.

After this, we looked at the established residential area and attempted to visualize the next logical areas that would develop. This became our residential zone.

The next phase was the easiest. We established agricultural zoning for those areas of Fairfield that were agricultural. This encompassed 90% of the entire area of the village.

With these basics in place, we had several more meetings at which we fine-tuned and honed the basic plan. By early Spring, we were ready to present the zoning ordinance to the community and, after several public hearings, the Zoning Ordinance was adopted and in place by the end of July 1955.

All of this activity and scrambling would lead one to believe that there was going to be a surge of development occurring within the Village, but such was not the case. There were few real estate offices in Fairfield at this time, and those few were home operations. The nearest source of real estate brokers and agents was in the City of Hamilton and, to them, the Village of Fairfield was anathema.

All of us who were associated with the Village spent a great deal of time trying to combat the stories that the real estate brokers were telling their customers. They were being told one or all of the following tales:

Taxes in Fairfield will be double those in Hamilton...
...the Village won't last....
...it will be 10 years before there are any utilities in the Village....
...there are no sewers, and those septic tanks will be a real health problem soon....
...fire protection is inadequate, and insurance rates will be very high....
...their Zoning Ordinance has not been tested, and you can't be sure what will be right next to you.

Our denials had little effect. Our only defense was to establish a record that belied those stories and that certainly couldn't, and didn't, happen overnight. Our later boom in development was a result of the establishment of the Fairfield Municipal Waterworks, the reliability of our Zoning Ordinance, and the fact that the City of Hamilton had no land that could be used for new residential subdivisions. When all of these factors were in place, the real estate boys and girls came by the score. Somehow, magically I'm sure, what had been a barren desert suddenly became the Promised Land, and there were Moses everywhere. Membership in the Pioneer Club grew into the hundreds.

Amazingly, many residents who had vigorously opposed incorporation turned up on the pioneer team.

At this point, I should tell you what being Mayor of Fairfield was like. When someone notes that you were the First Mayor of Fairfield now, some 47 years after the event, they envision you as a ribbon-cutter and custodian of the Key to the City.

It wasn't that way.

Until Paul Conrad was hired, I was not only the Chief Executive Officer of the municipality, I was the *only* executive officer. In addition to the ribbon-cutting, I was presiding at council meetings; working with the Treasurer and Solicitor in budgeting; working with the Solicitor in preparing necessary ordinances and resolutions to get the Village up and running; supervising all street repair and the Fire Department; representing the Village in all of the many legal situations—which were many at that time and disposing of dead animals. It was both a prestigious and humbling experience.

I also established a Mayor's Court, and heard many traffic and misdemeanor cases during my term. This court was the precursor of the Fairfield Municipal Court.

CHAPTER V

1955, Year of Triumph

As the year dawned, it was clear that if Fairfield were to survive, it must achieve two objectives:

1.) It must establish its credibility by performing in a satisfactory manner those services that every citizen is entitled to receive. That is, police protection, fire department services, public utilities, regulated zoning and development;

2.) It must preserve its boundaries for posterity. Living with the threat that vital municipal properties and inhabitants could be annexed to another city, or detached from the corporation into township status, precluded meaningful municipal status for Fairfield.

Proposition 2, being absolutely critical, soon demanded—and received—our rapt attention.

As the year began, there was pending before the Board of Butler County Commissioners a petition on which Joseph Hoelle was the agent, to annex to the Village of Fairfield eight sections (5,120 acres) of land. This was an area known as Stockton. It would prove to be an essential filing to the boundary integrity of the Fairfield municipality, as we shall see.

The first threat to the Village was a petition filed by Fannie and T.C. McGreevy seeking to annex to Hamilton 227.52 acres on the east side of Route 4, south of Symmes Road. The petition was heard by the County

Commissioners on January 10th. Carl Kollstedt, our Solicitor, and I appeared at the hearing opposing the annexation.

On January 17th, the Commissioners denied the petition by a vote of 2-1. The petititioners filed suit to set aside the Commissioner's decision. It was heard before Judge P.P. Boli on February 8, 1955. Carl Kollstedt and I appeared on behalf of the Village. Judge Boli took the matter under advisement and, somewhat later, upheld the action of the Commissioners in denying the petition.

The Village Council met on the evening of January 10th, and the *Journal News* carried the following account of the meeting on January 11, 1955:

First Budget Approved By Council Will Be Submitted to County Commission; Salaries of Officials Set; List Sources of Revenue

The Fairfield Village Council met Monday night in the Township House, Symmes Corner, and voted to submit a $94,300.00 budget to the Butler County Budget Commission. The budget—the first to be submitted by the new Council—"is based on estimated revenue within the 10-mill limitation in the sum of $66,200, which is based on a tax levy of 3.31 mills," reported Councilman Charles Vance, chairman of the Village Finance Committee.

"The figure $66,200 was computed by applying the estimated tax value of the property located within the Village limits at $21 million," Mr. Vance said. "The additional $10,000 will be derived from the 5-mill levy...for the benefit of the Fire Protection Fund of the Village, and this money can be used for the operation and maintenance of the fire department of the Village, including the

*payment of salaries for the firemen. This means that
there will be a total of $76,200 to be derived from monies
obtained by taxes on real property."*

Other Revenue

*The budget also includes estimated revenue of $6,000
from sales tax; $3,500 from liquor permits; $4,000 from
dealers intangible and financial institution taxes; $1,500
from fees and costs of ordinance cases; and miscellaneous
sources.*

*The Council received Mr. Vance's explanation that the
$10,000 from the fire protection levy can be used only for
fire equipment, maintenance and operating costs,
"which means that the amount of money available on
the estimated basis would be $84,300 for the general
operation of the Village."*

*The estimated expenses listed in the proposed budget
include: Council salaries, $720; mayor's salary, $2,400;
clerk's salary, $480.00; solicitor's salary, $1,800; police
chief's salary, $5,200; and salaries for four fulltime police
officers, $14,400.*

Additional Expenses

*Other expenses listed included: $12,900 for two police
cruisers, equipment, uniforms, jail care, and operating
expenses of police department; $20,000 for the fire
department, including salaries, new equipment, and
other department expenses; $12,000 for street repair,
including personal services, equipment and supplies;
$3,000 for street cleaning, including personal services and
other expenses; $2,000 for sewage and drainage; $2,850
contingent; and $7,200 for deductions by the county
auditor for the county health department, workmen's*

compensation, elections, auditor's and treasurer's fees, and other expenses.

"It is to be remembered that the amounts and figures appearing in this budget are in sharp contrast to the amount of money which the auditor's office of Butler County has advised us would be available during 1955," Mr. Vance stated. *"They have advised us that in their opinion the only money available would be the 1-Mill or $1 per $1,000 tax valuation currently being allocated to the Road and Bridge Fund of the township. We have based our figures on funds which should be available to us under the 10-mill levy.*

"In preparing the budget, we deducted first of all the1-mill currently being paid into the Road and Bridge Fund of the township. We then scrutinized the $2.80 available as free millage which was currently going to the schools, and it is our belief that the current needs of the Village are greater than those of the schools. However, in order to qualify for federal assistance, schools are required to have at least 10 mills allocated to them from taxes on real property. The current amount being paid to the school district is as follows: From taxes levied within the 10-mill limitation, $4.27; from levies outside the 10-mill limitation, $5.52; from free millage currently being delegated by the Budget Commission, $2.52—total $12.31.

"From this amount we have deducted 10 mills in order that our schools may still qualify for federal assistance. This leaves a balance of 2.31 mills, which could be available to the Village without depriving the schools of Federal Assistance."

Mayor Robert Wessel submitted his first report concerning affairs of the Village. In part, he said: "....We have been considering the facts in order to adopt the policy concerning detachment of territory from our Village by annexation to the City of Hamilton. We were faced with this problem immediately upon taking office, and it has been a factor of prime importance in Council work throughout the first two months of our term of office. We have met with the administrative officials of the City of Hamilton in an effort to work out a mutually satisfactory plan in this regard, but to date, we have reached no agreement.

"From the published reports of the meeting of the Council of the City of Hamilton in regard to this subject, it has been made to appear that our Council was dictating to the residents of the Village and attempting to deprive them of some of their democratic rights. I state unequivocally that this has not been, is not now, and never will be the policy of this Council.

Voluntary Choice

"It has been our policy," continued the mayor, "that should any segment of our Village wish to detach therefrom under conditions where these residents have a free and voluntary choice in the matter, our Council would take no action to prevent it. We do not believe, however, that the interests of democracy are served by subdividers who have no personal interest in the welfare of people who reside on the land which they are subdividing and whose only interest in attempting to detach the territory from the Village and annex it to the city is a monetary one.

"Nor do we believe that the interests of democracy are served when the new residents of the area are bound by a covenant in their deeds requiring them to sign annexation petitions. Obviously, we view with alarm any attempt to reduce the area of our Village, and we shall continue to resist these efforts wherever and whenever we are not satisfied that they express the desire of the majority of the residents involved....

"Our present plan is to establish our Mayor's Court some time during the month of January. It will be necessary for the solicitor and the mayor to meet with the Budget Commission of the county and to secure approval of our budget. A hearing on the application of the Village for a division of property and funds will be heard in February.

Under Handicap

"We have, of course, been severely handicapped by having no funds with which to operate, and as soon as the money is available we have many projects which require our immediate attention. These projects are repair of streets, employment of a marshall and Village police force, establishment of proper zoning for the Village area, and provisions for garbage disposal, to mention a few. Our success in this regard will be determined by the amount of money which is available to the Village.

"We believe that our Village is in as good a position at the present time as could be hoped for during the difficult period of organization. We believe that we will be successful in our efforts to provide the necessary requirements of the Village during the next year..." continued Mayor Wessel.

In connection with the annexation stand, Carl Lampl, vice president of the Fairfield Band and Orchestra Parents Association presented the following statement during the meeting:

"We, the members of the Fairfield Band and Orchestra Parents Association, wish to go on record stating that we disapprove of any more annexation from our Village which may cause us to lose the industry in our community. This would be a great detriment both to the community and the school, causing a severe hardship on the school."

Mayor Wessel read two letters he received from Hamilton City Manager Charles F. Schwalm. The first letter, in part, read: "I discussed with Hamilton City Council your council's ideas concerning a policy on pending and future annexations. Hamilton Council took the unanimous stand that they cannot accept any policy such as you expressed. They stated that it is not our present policy to solicit any annexation and all requests are brought by others. Council further stated that they feel it would not be within their right to make such a decision because they cannot bind future councils and it would thus be of no avail...."

The second letter from Mr. Schwalm read: "On Dec. 15, 1954, the City of Hamilton made request for permission to install water and electric lines to serve our water treatment plant on E. River Rd. We had already let contracts for these installations and had secured permission from the county to proceed according to plan. After your

*honorable body enacted legislation involving our com-
pletion of the project, the above permission request was
made and the work on the project was stopped.*

*"Our construction contracts had, of course, been
based on permits issued by the establishment of your
Village Council and we had no intimation that work
would not proceed according to the prearranged schedule. You can well understand that work stoppages under
these contracts already has involved this city in extra cost
under contract provision, and due to material shipments
and labor commitments. If prolonged further, the extra
cost will become more and more.*

*"Therefore, may we have your decision in this matter
at the earliest possible date? Inasmuch as I understand
your Council meets this evening (January 10, 1955), we
earnestly request that you consider this matter and allow
us to proceed on these urgently needed improvements."*

*Mayor Wessel stated that the first letter required no
action, and he referred the second letter to the Planning
Committee for consideration.*

The foregoing report is really a summary of events for the Village of
Fairfield in January 1955.

The adopted policy of the Village was to resist all attempts to remove
territory.

On January 20, 1955, John C. Hicks filed a petition to detach from
the Village of Fairfield and to annex to the City of Hamilton fifty acres.
It included some territory contained in the McGreevy Petition, the area
now known as Hicks Manor Shopping Center and many residential
sites surrounding the Center.

This petition was rejected by the Butler County Commissioners.

On January 3rd at a special council meetings, I named the people appointed to the Planning Commission and Screening Committee to screen job applicants for the Village.

On the same date, the Butler County Commissioners were checking the names on the Hoelle Petition to annex the 10-square mile and proposed addition to the Village.

On February 1st, council of the City of Hamilton unanimously approved annexation of the Hammond Subdivision after the Village's suit to enjoin the proceedings had failed.

The question of constructing a municipal waterworks was not so easily solved. None of us had any experience in constructing or operating a municipal waterworks, and we were all novices when it came to financing the construction. We had several meetings with bonding company officials who did their best to explain to us how we could issue mortgage revenue bonds and pay for the systems without any increases in taxes.

We talked, listened and discussed. We invited anyone who seemed to have any expertise to help us. We were indeed floundering until suddenly upon the scene came C.L. Snyder, Nelson Watson and various other associates. These men were professionals who had traveled these routes before, and in short order, we had a plan.

The February 15th edition of the *Journal-News*, the column banner, *"Fairfield Council Authorizes Water System Study"*, related:

$2,500 Cost of Preliminary Survey Will Be Financed By
Revenue Bonds; Propose Sewer System to Be Paid By Special
Assessments

The Fairfield Village Council met Monday night in the Township Fire House, Symmes Corner, and approved a preliminary study of a proposed waterworks system for the village. The study, expected to be completed in 30-45 days, will be made by an Indiana engineering firm, and if approved by the Council—and without any major interruption to the work—the waterworks system could be completed by fall, according to C.L. Snyder of Snyder, McLellan and Watson, engineers, Hillsboro, Ind.

The cost of the preliminary study will be about $2,500, none of which will be payable by the village should the group decide against installing the waterworks system. Should the preliminary study show such a water plan to be feasible in the village, the project would be financed by revenue bonds issued by the Council and purchased by Nelson Browning and Co., Cincinnati, an investment securities firm. The revenue bonds would be paid off from revenue received from water consumers in the village, over a 40-year period at 3-1/2 per cent interest.

The study also will include the feasibility of a sewer system in the village. This proposal, if approved by the village and by the residents to be served by the sewer system, would require special assessments. These special assessments cannot be levied without the approval of Council and without the approval of those to be assessed.

Also, in the course of the same article, it was reported:

The Council voted to appeal the decision of the Butler County Budget Commission to the State Board of Tax Appeals. The County Commission recently advised that the Village could expect only $11,000 in tax money for

*1955 operating expenses, whereas the Council had sub-
mitted a budget for $84,000.*

On March 25th, the Butler County Commissioners set the hearing
on the George Washington School annexation for May 24th.

On the same date, the *Journal-News* carried an article and architect's
sketch of a general office building, which Champion International
(then Champion Paper and Fibre Company) was going to construct in
the Village.

On March 28th, Fairfield Council discussed the matter and voted to
send a letter to Champion Paper and Fibre Company, welcoming them
to the Village and offering every assistance when they moved their general offices to Fairfield. The site was to be where the present Fairfield
City Building stands.

On April 11th, the Butler County Commissioners unanimously
approved the Hoelle Petition for annexation of 5,120 acres of land in
the Stockton area to the Village. The *Journal-News* of April 12th, in
part, reported:

> *"A 60-day waiting period will be required before
> Fairfield Village Council can take action on the annexa-
> tion of 5,120 acres of land in the Stockton area approved
> Tuesday by Butler County Commissioners, Gordon
> Augsberger, president of the Board said Wednesday.*
>
> *"The territory extends from the village corporation
> line along Rte. 4 (Dixie Hwy.) to the Butler-Hamilton
> County line, eastward to the Union Township line, north
> to Tylersville Rd., and west to the eastern boundary of
> Gilmore Rd. thence to the east boundary of Winton Rd.,
> and south to the county line.*

"Some opposition to the proposed measure was voiced Tuesday by residents attending the hearing although the majority present favored the move.

"In opposing the proposed annexation, Mrs. Esther Benzing, 3051 Mack Rd., told the Board that 'the issues are not clear,' and that she wanted a further explanation of the matter. 'I don't believe that some persons signing the petition fully understood the meaning of the proposal,' she said. She pointed out that most of the area contains farm land and that in her opinion many of the land owners are satisfied to remain out of the village.

"Warren Rieser, 3301 Tylersville Rd., also voiced his disapproval of the proposed annexation. He explained that 'farmers in the area cannot afford to pay the village taxes which will be a third higher.'"

Fairfield water was the topic of the public meeting held on May 4th. The *Journal-News* reported:

"About 150 persons Thursday night attended an informative meeting concerning the proposed Village of Fairfield Waterworks, held in Fairfield Township High School Auditorium under the sponsorship of the Fairfield Residents Association. William Holden, representing the Association, was moderator for the program.

"Thirty-five applications for water from the planned waterworks were signed after the meeting ended; nearly two hours were spent on questions and answers on the subject.

"Questions were answered by Mayor Robert Wessel, C.L. Snyder, municipal accountant, and Nelson Watson, engineer."

Probate Judge, Harry F. Walsh, divided the property between the Village of Fairfield and Fairfield Township in an opinion issued May 4th. The *Journal-News* reported:

> *"Division of fire department funds and equipment between the Fairfield Township trustees and the Village of Fairfield, effective June 1, is ordered in an opinion handed down today by Probate Judge Harry F. Walsh.*
>
> *"The proceedings involve division of fire department property and monies received from a $13,000 fire protection levy, so that both the newly-incorporated village of Fairfield and the remaining Fairfield Township will have proper fire protection.*
>
> *"Last Dec. 10, the village had filed application with the Probate Court for division of the funds with subsequent hearings on Feb. 16 and March 9."*
>
> *Opinion Given*
>
> *"In the opinion, Judge Walsh stated, "The Court believes that it would be equitable and for the best interest of all the people of the areas involved that No. 2 Fire House located on U.S. Rte. 127 (at Symmes Corner) and the Township House located there be transferred to the Village of Fairfield, and that the Township House and Fire House No. 1 on Tylersville Rd. be allowed to remain in the name of the Fairfield Township Trustees.*
>
> *"The judge further found that fire trucks and equipment located at the respective fire houses be transferred as follows: All trucks and equipment in No. 2 Fire House be transferred to the Village of Fairfield, and all trucks and equipment in No. 1 Fire House be kept in the name of the trustee.*

"At the same time the annual levy now being collected in the amount of $13,000 which is paid to the Fairfield Township Trustees for the benefit of all the people in the township (including the village) for fire protection, is ordered divided on a basis of 55 per cent to the Village of Fairfield and 45 per cent to Fairfield Township, beginning on June 1.

"The Court instructs the clerk of the township to pay over to the Village of Fairfield 55 per cent of all monies in the fire fund as of June 1 and all monies here and after received from the collection of the levy during the remaining life of the levy. The levy was passed in 1952, and will expire in 1956.

"Any obligations as of June 1 against the fire fund shall be paid first before any division of the fund is made, the Court rules.

"After this date, the Village of Fairfield will have its own fire department and will be obligated to pay all charges for fire protection out of its proportionate share of the fire fund, as ordered distributed by the Probate Court.

"Judge Walsh suggested that the village and township enter into negotiations immediately as to fire protection in their respective districts, so that the equipment which has been purchased and paid for by Fairfield Township residents can be used by both political subdivisions.

Transfer Property

"The Court also found that certain property located at the No. 2 Fire House at Symmes Corner is township-owned and will be transferred to the township trustees.

"This includes township road equipment and office equipment used by the Fairfield Township trustees in meeting place.

"The Court suggested the possibility, however, that some agreement might be reached between the village and township as to the use of the equipment until the village is able to purchase and maintain its own road building department.

"Judge Walsh ordered the division of property effective June 1, and directed an entry be drawn accordingly carrying out the provisions of the opinion."

On May 19th, a petition seeking reversion of 1500 acres of Village territory to township status was filed by Oakley Wooten. *Journal-News* synopsis follows:

"A petition seeking a special election on the question of detachment of 1,500 acres of territory north of Nilles Rd. in the Village of Fairfield, and returning the area to township status was filed late Thursday afternoon with the Butler County Board of Elections.

"Containing 348 signatures of residents of the area, the petition was submitted by Oakley Wooten, 2613 Bobmyer Rd., chairman of the Fairfield Township Reorganization Committee.

"J. Earl Gray, deputy clerk of the Board of Elections, explained Friday that the signatures on the petition must be checked in order to determine whether it contains the signatures of 15 per cent of registered voters in the area. Mr. Gray said that he could not estimate the number of residents in the area sought for detachment at this time.

Special Election

"Under Ohio law the Board of Elections must order a special election on the question of detachment whenever

it is presented with a petition signed by 15 per cent of the voters.

"According to the Board official about 10 days will be required to check the validity of the names contained on the petition and then another 20 days before an election can be ordered.

"The territory involved in the detachment proposal includes all village land north of Nilles Rd., including all Village Precinct A, a greater portion of Precinct B, a section of Precinct C at Symmes Corner and portions of Lindale and Riverdale Subdivisions in Precinct D.

"Area boundaries extend east along Bobmyer Rd. to Gilmore Rd., south on Gilmore to Hamilton-Carthage Rd., then west on a line along Nilles Rd. to Muskopf Rd., north from Muskopf to the Great Miami River then eastward again paralleling the Hamilton corporation limits on the north."

May 24 and 25 presented difficult days for the Village.

On May 24th, the Board of Elections was checking the signatures on a petition to detach territory from the village filed by Oakley Wooten as agent. The petition sought to detach from the Village all that area lying north of Nilles Road. It included the Fisher Body Plant, and all other industrial property within the village. If approved by the voters, it would be disastrous to the Village.

On May 25th, the Butler County Commissioners approved the annexation by the City of Hamilton of the 127.28 acre tract, a part of which was the site of the present George Washington Junior High School.

Journal-News of May 25th proclaimed:

BULLETIN

The Butler County Board of Elections early Wednesday afternoon set Tuesday, June 14, as the date of a special election to determine whether a section of Fairfield Village is to revert to township status. The board found the detachment petition adequate.

Butler County Commissioners at 4:10 p.m. Tuesday approved the annexation of 127.28 acres of Fairfield Village land to the City of Hamilton, and this was followed by an immediate statement from village officials to the effect that the decision would be appealed to the Common Pleas Court.

The 127.28 acres as approved for annexation is bounded by St. Clair Ave. on the north, Pleasant Ave. on the west, Symmes Rd. on the south, and the school boundary line on the east. It includes the new George Washington Junior High School, along with all of the roadway on Symmes and Pleasant, within the boundaries involved.

May Set Voting Date

At the same time, another matter affecting Fairfield Village was scheduled to come before the Board of Elections Wednesday afternoon.

Board workers late Tuesday completed their check of signatures contained on a petition calling for the detachment of a 1,500 acre tract in the village north of Nilles Rd., this territory to revert to township status.

Harry Grevey, chairman of the Board of Elections, said that a special meeting is scheduled Wednesday afternoon, at which time the petition will be studied and possibly a date for the election set.

Must Wait 60 Days

The annexation of the Junior High territory, which must now remain tabled for 60 days before submission to the Hamilton City Council for action, was given approval after the Board of Commissioners determined that maps and the description of the territory involved agreed.

Mayor Robert F. Wessel and Carl Kollstedt, solicitor, both representing the village, had stated at Tuesday's public hearing that the petition contained inaccuracies, and was not correctly filed at the office of R.H. Smith, county auditor.

The Commissioners ordered Jesse Pochard, county engineer, to recheck the maps available and the description of the territory which was published as a legal advertisement as required by law.

Papers Found Correct

The county engineer found that the description as filed and advertised was adequate.

At the same time, the Board of Elections found the Wooten Petition to contain an adequate number of qualified signatures, and set the election thereon for Tuesday, June 14th.

Will Decide If 1,500-Acre Village Tract To
Return to Township Status

"The Butler County Board of Elections Wednesday afternoon set Tuesday, June 14, as the date for a special election on the question of detachment of a 1,500-acre

tract north of Nilles Rd. from the newly incorporated Village of Fairfield, after acceptance of a petition filed by Fred Randolph, attorney for Oakley Wooten, 2613 Bobmyer Rd., agent for the petitioners.

"If the detachment issue is approved by voters, the area would revert back to Fairfield Township. All registered voters in the area proposed to be detached are eligible to vote in the special election whether they are property owners or not.

"A quorum made up of Harry B. Grevey, chairman of the Elections Board, George H. Brandoff, and James E. Shollenbarger, member, approved the special election date following a check of signatures on the detachment petition Tuesday by Board of Elections workers. Martin A. Coyle, the other board member, is out of the city, and was not present at the meeting.

229 Valid Signatures

"The board found the petition to be adequate in that 229 of the 348 signatures were valid. It was determined that 1,249 persons are now eligible to vote in the area proposed for detachment, with the petition needing only 15 per cent or 188 signatures of registered voters.

"Mr. Randolph late Tuesday afternoon had posted with the board a $500 check which will be used to defray expenses of the special election.

"At the same time, the board announced the deadline for voters in the detachment area to register for the special election has been set at Saturday, noon, June 4, or 10 days before the election as required by law. Only persons living in the proposed detachment area may cast ballots.

"At Wednesday's meeting, Ben Worcester, Middletown attorney and clerk of the Board of Elections, J. Earl Gray, *deputy clerk, Mr. Randolph, attorney for the petitioners, and Carl Kollstedt, Fairfield Village solicitor, were in attendance with the board members.*

"Mr. Kollstedt, as solicitor for the village and attorney for Robert Wessel.

"Mayor Wessel's objections read, in part:

"As mayor of the Village of Fairfield, and in my individual capacity of a resident and taxpayer within the affected area, I hereby wish to raise the following objections to the petition filed herein, and request the Board to bar the petition for the following reasons:

"There is now pending before the County Commissioners a petition to annex 127.28 acres to the City of Hamilton from the Village of Fairfield, all of which territory is included within the area embraced by the petition for detachment of territory before this honorable body.

"That said election, if allowed, would be contrary to the laws and Constitution of the State of Ohio."

Mayor Wessel's statement declared that "where more than one petition has been filed with a board or tribunal seeking the annexation or detachment of the same or parts of the same territory, that to which jurisdiction to act first attaches is entitled to precedence, and no action can be taken on the others during the pendency of the proceeding upon the petition so entitled to give precedence.

Asks Action Deferred

"He asked that the board defer action on the detachment petition until there has been a final determination of rights on the annexation petition now pending.

"The annexation of the 127.28 acre tract around the new George Washington Junior High School, just off Symmes Rd., must wait 60 days before the measure is submitted to Hamilton City Council for its approval.

"The Board of Elections accepted the list of objections for file, but it was explained by this body that it has no power to determine what effect, if any, it would have on the election matter.

"It was pointed out that the board must accept the (detachment) petition if the signatures were sufficient and valid.

"The board deferred action on establishing a possible site for the special election, until it could determine a central location for the polling places. Whether voters in the proposed detachment area would use the Symmes Corner fire house, as in the past, has not been determined at present.

Asks Central Location

"Mr. Randolph suggested to the Board that a more centrally located site might be advisable, since voters in the extreme eastern section of the area also are involved. He explained that the fire house, located on Mt. Pleasant Pk (US Route 127) is located in the extreme southwestern part of the detachment area, in what he termed the "heart of the opposition."

"Mr. Grevey, Board chairman, conceded this, but explained that the success or failure of such an election would not necessarily depend upon the location of the voting places."

These two decisions caused a fury within the Village. First and foremost, we had to rally the troops to defeat the Wooten Petition for detachment and annexation. Were it to succeed, we would be a village in name only.

Concurrently, we had to prepare our appeal to the George Washington Junior High decision.

On May 30th, Carl Kollstedt, on behalf of the Village of Fairfield, filed suit to enjoin the special election June 14th on the grounds that the voters in the George Washington Junior High area should not be permitted to vote for the reason that annexation of the Washington tract has already been approved by the Butler County Commissioners.

On June 4th, Judge Fred B. Cramer dismissed the injunction suit permitting the June 14th election to proceed. We immediately appealed this decision to the 1st District Court of Appeals. The Court set the case for hearing on June 13th at 11:00 a.m. The Appeals Court heard the matter and, just after noon, made its decision upholding Judge Cramer.

The eligible voters went to the polls on June 14th and, fortunately, defeated the Wooten Petition by 189 votes. The *Journal-News* on June 15th reported, in part:

PLAN DEFEATED BY 189-VOTE MAJORITY

Area North of Nilles Road
Remains in Village

70.6 Per Cent
Of Electors In 1,500 Acre Section
Case Ballots;
Vote is 720 to 531

Residents of a 1,500-acre area north of Nilles Rd. in Fairfield Village, by a decisive 720 to 531 vote, defeated a proposed measure for detachment of that territory from the village in a special election Tuesday in four village precincts. Thus the detachment proposal was defeated by a margin of 189 votes.

The election was a victory for village officials who earlier had sought to enjoin the Butler County Board of Elections from proceedings with the balloting. Their injunction suit, filed by Robert F. Wessel, mayor of Fairfield Village, and Carl M. Kollstedt, village solicitor, had been dismissed by Common Pleas Judge Fred B. Cramer and the local court's decision was upheld Monday of this week by the First District Court of Appeals in Cincinnati.

Retains Present Area

As a result of the election, the village will retain its present area, although a smaller 127.28-acre tract located around the new George Washington Junior High School is currently pending annexation to the City of Hamilton.

Ben Worcester, Middletown clerk of the Board of Elections, pointed out that the 1,251 votes cast represented 70.6 per cent of the eligible voters in the area proposed for detachment. A majority affirmation vote of 626 in favor of the detachment issue would have been needed for passage of the measure, or a switch of 95 ballots cast on the detachment issue.

To Certify Results

Board of Elections officials will certify the results of the special election and transmit them to Ted W. Brown, Ohio Secretary of State, probably on Thursday when the board meets to place their signatures on the certification.

The Village was saved again.

On Wednesday, June 15th, at a special meeting, council of the Village of Fairfield approved annexation of the Stockton area.

This was vital to the survival of the municipality. It assured that the area would have at least 5000 residents so as to become a city, and it finally fixed the boundaries of the Village/City.

The report of the *Journal-News* on July 15th is succinct and covers all the points:

Fairfield Council Approves Annexation of Stockton Area

5,120-Acre Section, With 700 Population, May Put Village in City Status; Request For Census To Be Made To Federal Bureau

---

The Fairfield Village Council met Wednesday night in special session, in the Village Fire House, Symmes Corner, and voted 5-1 in favor of accepting for annexation 5,120 acres in the Stockton area. The new section, containing about 700 persons, increases the Village population to an estimated 5,500 and places the Village in a city status. Councilman Charles Vance voted against the annexation.

On June 27th, the Village Council ordered a Federal Census of the Village. The *Journal-News* reported:

The Fairfield Village Council met Monday night in the Village Fire House, Symmes Corner, and voted authority to Mayor Robert Wessel to order a census of the Village by the Bureau of Census, Washington. It was *reported that the cost will be about $1,500 and Mayor Wessel will furnish maps of the area to the Bureau's office in Chicago, from where the census takers will be assigned.*

The purpose of the census is to determine whether the Village has a population of 5,000 or more, a figure neces- sary to give the area its sought-after city status. The Council recently approved the annexation of about 700 residents in the Stockton area to the Village, a move thought to be sufficient to give the community the required 5,000 population and thereby halt the threat of future detachments from the Village.

At the end of July, Carl Kollstedt and I, representing Will C. Dreher, filed suit to enjoin the City of Hamilton from annexing the George Washington school area. Judge Cramer set the matter for hearing on August 8th, and on that date, the matter was heard by visiting Judge Louis J. Schneider on assignment from Hamilton County.

After three hours of hearing, the matter was recessed until August 9th, at which time the hearing was completed and the injunction was denied. The decision was appealed to the First District Court of Appeals, and the appeal was denied on September 2, 1955. This cleared the way for the City of Hamilton to complete the annexation, which it did on September 7, 1955.

On August 24th, the Fairfield Council awarded a contract to the Coleman, Trainor Company of Huntington, West Virginia, for the con- struction of a waterworks for the sum of $689,567.11. Work was to begin within thirty days.

Also on this date, John C. Hicks filed a petition to detach 340.65 acres. This was an area bounded on the north by Symmes Road, on the south by Nilles Road, on the west by Anthony Wayne Avenue, and on the east by Route 4 (Dixie Highway). It was set for hearing before the Butler County Commissioners on November 4th. It would be resisted.

The Federal Census of the Village was underway on August 30th. On September 6th, the *Journal-News* announced:

Fairfield Census Nets City Status
Population Figure of 6,182 Announced; Includes
Residents of Annexing Areas

Robert Wessel, mayor of Fairfield Village, announced Tuesday that unofficial returns of the census enumeration conducted last week in the Village show a population of 6,182 residents, or about 400 more than estimated. The census was ordered by the Village Council to determine if the area had the necessary 5,000 residents to achieve city status, and this figure has been reached.

Mayor Wessel said an official total will not be known for several weeks. He reported that formal word on the census will not be received for about a month, and then the Ohio Secretary of State will be notified of the results, and if found to be more than 5,000, the Village will have a 30-day waiting period before it formally reaches city status. "I expect it will be at least two months before we officially become a city," continued the mayor.

Governmental Changes

Eventually there will probably be a change in the government set-up, he added, with the residents being given the choice of several types of government, including the city manager-council and the mayor-council form of government.

*The census, when officially announced, will halt fur-
ther detachments from the Village, said Mayor Wessel,
and will permit the Council to devote full time to internal rather than external problems. The new status also
will return more motor vehicle and gasoline taxes to the
area, according to the mayor.*

*Fairfield Village, with an area of 23 square miles, is
expected to be one of the largest cities in the state, in area.*

*"The Council and I wish to thank all of the residents
for their cooperation with the census enumerators," said
the mayor, "and those who were not listed in the census
may still do so. Interested persons should contact me or a
member of the Council."*

*The census just completed included those residents liv-
ing in the three areas now being considered for annexation to Hamilton; the George Washington Junior High
School area, the River Road area, and about 300 acres
along Rte. 4 or Dixie Hwy. "Should these detachments
from the Village be made", said Mr. Wessel, "they will not
change the results of the census as far as Fairfield reaching city status."*

On September 15th, Warren Reiser, as agent for the petitioners and
Mark Brown and Lester Koehler as attorneys, filed a petition with the
Board of Elections seeking to detach 4,700 acres of the Village and
return it to township status. The area included all the Village industry
and the Fairfield Township School. It was big trouble.

The *Journal-News* on September 16th reported:

*Butler County Board of Elections officials Friday
morning were checking some 78 names on a petition filed
late Thursday afternoon at the Board office in the*

Courthouse seeking detachment of approximately 4,200 acres from Fairfield Village and the return of the area to Fairfield township status.

J. Earl Gray, deputy clerk of the Board, said Friday that if the petition contains signatures equal to 15 per cent of the total votes cast in the territory at the last general election, a special election must be called within 20 days after the petition is declared valid. About 125 persons reside in the area, Mr. Gray said. A simply majority vote is required for passage of the measure.

Area Outlined

The proposed detachment area, which includes the Hamilton Fisher Body plant, American Cyanimid Co., Associate Aircraft-Tool & Manufacturing, Inc., and the Fairfield Township School, extends from Bobmyer and Tuley Rds., eastward to Gilmore Rd., then northward to Tylersville Rd., and eastward on Tylersville to the east boundary of Fairfield Village.

The boundary then runs southward to the Baltimore & Ohio Railroad, northwesterly to Port Union Rd., southwesterly to Rte. 4 (Dixie Hwy.); and Gilmore Rd., northward on Gilmore to the railroad, then back to Rte. 4 just south of Fairfield School. It follows Dixie Hwy. northward to a point north of the railroad underpass and then swings eastwardly to the point of its beginning.

The petition was filed by Mark Brown and Lester Koehler, Hamilton attorneys. Warren Reiser, 3301 Tylersville Rd., has been listed as agent for the petitioners.

The Board found the petition contained sufficient signatures of registered voters and set a special election for October 4th. The following synopsis was reported by the *Hamilton-Journal* on September 26th:

DETACHMENT VOTE SET OCTOBER 4TH
Call Special Election to Decide Whether Fairfield
Tract Reverts to Twp. Status

A special election on the proposed detachment of a 4,200-acre tract from the Village of Fairfield and return of the territory to township status has been ordered for Tuesday, Oct. 4, following approval Monday afternoon by the Butler County Board of Elections of a petition filed by residents of the area.

J. Earl Gray, deputy clerk of the Board, said Tuesday that the petition was found to contain signatures of 63.3 per cent of registered voters in the area who cast ballots in the last general election. Fifteen per cent was required to place the issue before the voters in the special election, he added.

Deadline Friday

At the same time, Mr. Gray explained that the Board had set registration deadline for the special election for Friday. He said that there are now 106 persons residing in the area who are properly registered to vote.

The Friday registration deadline for the special election was set in accordance with law which requires it to be 10 days before the balloting.

Polls will be established at Fairfield Township School for the special election and only registered voters residing in the area proposed for detachment will be eligible to vote, the deputy clerk pointed out.

The Board of Elections ordered necessary ballots printed for the election.

Voice Objections

Objections to the proposed detachment were voiced by Fairfield Village officials who attended Monday's meeting of the Board.

Robert F. Wessel, mayor of the village, and Carl M. Kollstedt, village solicitor, contended that the detachment petition is contrary to law in that the area includes a section which had been involved in another special election for detachment less than a year ago. At that time voters of the area defeated a move to detach from the Village.

Both Mr. Wessel and Mr. Kollstedt announced that action would be taken in Common Pleas Court in an effort to halt the election. They said preparations were now underway.

The village officials also opposed the proposed detachment on the grounds that an accurate map or plat was not filed with the petition, that it does not contained sufficient signatures, and that the area involved territory now included in an annexation petition and that the village had obtained city status.

Await Official Notice

No official notice of the recent census in Fairfield Village can be taken by the Board of Elections until it is officially declared to be a city by Secretary of State Ted W. Brown, officials said. A 30-day waiting period must also follow the secretary's certification, Jackson Bosch, prosecutor, told the Board.

The detachment petition was signed by 65 residents of the area, 55 of whom were determined to be registered voters. About 125 persons reside in the territory of which 106 are now registered voters.

The petition was filed by Mark Brown and Lester Koehler, Hamilton attorneys, listing Warren Reiser, 3301 Tylersville Rd., as agent for the petitioners.

On September 27th, the Village of Fairfield by Robert F. Wessel, Mayor, and Carl Kollstedt, as solicitor, and with Helen Wessel, a resident taxpayer, filed suit to enjoin the election.

Concurrently, we alerted the Fairfield Residents Association to wage a campaign within the area to get voters to vote against detachment. We met with many signers of the petition and assured them that, upon their request, the council would detach their property and have it revert to Township status if they would vote against detachment. The petition was set for hearing on Tuesday, September 27th, before Judge Fred B. Cramer, and on that date a temporary injunction was denied. This meant that the October 4th election would proceed. The election was held on October 4th, and the report of the *Journal-News* on October 5th dramatically shows what a squeaker it was.

It reported:

Fairfield Village residents in a special election Tuesday rejected by a 59 to 52 vote a move for detachment of a 4,200 acre tract from the village and return it to township status.

A total of 111 voters out of 126 eligibles or nearly 89 per cent, went to the polls located in the lobby of Fairfield School auditorium. A majority affirmative vote of 56 would have been required for passage of the detachment measure on the basis of 111 votes.

As a result of the election, the territory will retain its present village status.

Fewer Than Signers

The number voting for detachment (52) was 13 fewer than the number of signatures on the detachment petition filed by Warren Reiser, 3301 Tylersville Rd., as agent for petitioners.

At the time of filing, Butler County Board of Elections officials had determined that 55 of the 65 persons signing the petition had been registered voters.

The affirmative vote, percentage-wise was 46.9 for the proposed detachment, with 53.1 per cent against the detachment.

When we learned the results of the election on the question of detachment, we began to wonder if some of the electors in the area hadn't hedged their bets since even though we said we would allow them to withdraw, it was better to be safe than sorry.

On October 10th, the Fairfield Village Council met and, true to its commitment, approved detachment of 3,200 acres of the 4,200 acres that had sought detachment.

The *Journal-News* reported:

The Fairfield Village Council met Monday night in the Village Municipal Bldg., Symmes Corner, and approved detachment of about 3,200 acres of land from the village which reverts to township status. Twenty-four farms are involved. The Butler County Commissioners will act on the detachment this week.

The area approved for detachment includes land within the following boundaries: Mulhauser Rd. and B&O R.R. north to Tylersville Rd., west to Gilmore Rd., south to intersection of Gilmore and Port Union Rd., east to north side of B&O R.R., southeast on railroad to south line of section 15, and east to point of beginning.

> *Approval by the Council follows agreement announced by the members several weeks ago, permitting detachment of any Village farmland adjacent to the Township, upon request of the property owners. The land involved was originally part of the 4,200 acre tract subject to vote last Tuesday, when residents in the area voted 59 to 52 against detachment. The 3,200-acre tract approved for detachment Monday night does not include any industries or Fairfield School.*

The Village, once again, was saved and, with the exception of the outstanding Hicks detachment area, the boundaries were secure since our advance to city status was only a few days away.

Also only a few days away was the municipal election, including the election of the first Fairfield City Council and other officers. On October 18th, County Prosecutor, Jack Bosch, reported that he had received an opinion from the Ohio Attorney General that opined that all Fairfield offices for the new city would have to be filled by write-in-ballot.

The opinion stated, in part:

> "No names of persons who have been nominated or have filed nominating petitions for office of the pre-existent village are entitled to be placed on the ballot for such offices at any succeeding election," the attorney general ruled.

Bosch explained that none of the nominating petitions filed by 14 candidates for village offices were valid, and none of these persons named would appear on the ballot.

Attorney General O'Neil further stated:

In his opinion, Mr. O'Neil said the first thing which must be done is to divide the new city into wards. This, he said, must be accomplished before the election.

Electors in the new city will elect a mayor for a two-year term, a president of council for a two-year term, an auditor for two years, a solicitor for two years, a treasurer for two years, and seven councilmen who also will serve two-year terms. Four of the councilmen are to be elected from the wards and three will serve as councilmen-at-large.

"The officers of a village serving at the time of its transition to the status of a city may continue to serve as such officers until the election and qualification of city officials but may exercise only the powers given by law to village officers," the attorney general stated.

The Fairfield Village Council met with Jackson Bosch, reviewed the opinion and announced that they would meet on Monday, October 24th, to establish four city wards.

On October 20, 1955, Secretary of State Ted W. Brown issued a proclamation declaring Fairfield to officially be a city. The final tally by the Federal Census Bureau found that 6,202 persons resided within the city.

This set off a gala salute to Fairfield, with a program and dinner on the very day Fairfield became a city. This event was sponsored by the Fairfield Resident's Association.

On October 23rd, the *Journal-News* reported *"Sidelights As City Is Born"*.

It follows:

Fairfield officials seated at a center table in the spacious cafeteria had a momentary fright and then minutes of hilarious fun when Solicitor Carl Kollstedt showed them the certification of the recent detachment vote held in Fairfield. The certification, signed by all members of the Butler County Board of Elections, reads: "For detachment, 59; against detachment 52."

Actually, the results of the detachment vote were just the opposite, but the erratic certification seemed to be a fitting climax to the community's efforts for a city. Said one official, "Everything else has happened. There is no reason why the certification shouldn't be wrong." The certification will be corrected.

The tables were decorated with beautiful ivy and flowers, and the speakers' table also included attractive lighted candles. Novel souvenir items were miniature copies of the Secretary of State's proclamation, certifying that Fairfield is a city.

Custer Reynolds, toastmaster, conveyed greetings from the guests to George Zimmers, clerk of the Village, who is ill and was unable to attend. Mr. Zimmers has been an active supporter of the new government, and has devoted many hours toward its successful conclusion.

The pageant represented considerable attention by members of the school faculty, the students, and William J. Vogelgesang, who was in charge of dramatics; Earl F. Kinker, music; and Betzy Schul, the talented accompanist. This flash-back of early Fairfield history included a live chicken and a dog.

Mr. Reynolds, who did an outstanding job as toastmaster, related the story of the southern moonshiners riding a train for the first time, and enjoying their first bottle of soft drink. As one of the moonshiners took his first sip, the train passed through a dark tunnel. When asked by the second mountaineer how the soft drink tasted, the first moonshiner replied, "Don't touch the stuff, I've just been struck blind!"

Guests introduced by the toastmaster included Butler County Prosecutor, Jackson Bosch, County Commissioners Gordon Augspurger, Ben Van Gordon, and Arthur Reiff; Common Pleas Judge Fred B. Cramer, County Engineer Jesse Pochard, Sheriff Charles B. Walke, all members of Fairfield Council and the officers; Robert Cropenbaker, superintendent of Fairfield Schools; Jack Dougherty, president of Fairfield Civitan Club; Richard Block, representing Fairfield Grange; Jack McCormick, fire chief; Warren Steele of the Fairfield Civic Association; Cpl. D.A. Girton of the State Highway Field Farm Bureau, who was unable to attend but sent his best wishes; members of the press and radio staffs, and others.

Dr. Arthur F. Schalk, chairman of the Fairfield Residents Committee, presented a souvenir wooden key to the city to Mayor Robert Wessel, which will be displayed in the City Municipal Bldg., Symmes Corner.

When introducing Mayor Arthur Fiehrer, Mr. Reynolds said: "The city to our north is one of the most industrialized cities in the nation....When faced by adversities they have been able to overcome those problems...It makes it a most desirable place to live."

The delicious dinner included turkey, dressing, peas, sweet potatoes, slaw, tomato juice, coffee, hot rolls, butter, cranberry sauce, and ice cream. The serving was ably handled by the Orchestra and Band Parents Club and students.

The entire program was a masterful piece of planning. Though lengthy in printed size, the festivities were conducted with a minimum of lost effort, and held the attention of the large audience throughout the evening.

Dr. Schalk closed the evening with most appropriate remarks: "The village has gone. A new city has arisen. Long live Fairfield!"

On October 25th, the Butler County Commissioners, Gordon Augspurger and Arthur Reiff, heard the petition of John C. Hicks to detach 340.65 acres from the former village, now City of Fairfield. Over 100 persons attended the hearing, after which the petition was rejected. The boundaries were now totally intact and preserved.

The same day, Fairfield Council established four wards to comply with the opinion of the Attorney General and Secretary of State.

Since I hoped to continue to be mayor of Fairfield, I wanted to get that fact before the voters. The election was on November 8th. It was already October 27th. The Fairfield Resident's Association under the direction of Grace Hoelle announced they would publish a listing of all persons seeking municipal office. I registered my name with the Resident's Association then, other than working the polls on Election Day, there was nothing to do but wait. Mrs. Hoelle announced on Saturday, October 29th, that 29 candidates had announced with the Resident's Association. The list included twenty candidates for council, two for mayor, two for treasurer, one for solicitor, and two for President of Council.

Election Day, November 8th, came and passed. The pertinent results:

MAYOR

Robert F. Wessel	1141
Warren Steele	460

AUDITOR

Grace Hoelle	1076
Jack Gase	267

TREASURER

Winifred Field	947
Ralph Schwab	505

SOLICITOR

Carl Kollstedt	1315

PRESIDENT OF COUNCIL

Larry Lloyd	770
*Robert Mansfield	368

COUNCILMAN AT LARGE (3 to be elected)

William Holden	885
Walter Hunter	873
Ellis Muskopf	789
*Kenneth Faist	342

COUNCILMAN 1ST WARD

Francis J. Miller	232
Joe Kuntz	202

COUNCILMAN 2ND WARD

Charles Vance	145
Fred Klamo	87

COUNCILMAN 3RD WARD

Ben Groh	146
Walter M. Fath	110

COUNCILMAN 4TH WARD

Merle Daugherty	167
Carl Lampl	5

Kenneth Faist and Robert Mansfield did not seek new terms.

About 1700 voters went to the polls. Robert Wessel, Winifred Field, Carl Kollstedt, Walter Hunter, Ellis Muskopf, Charles Vance and Ben Groh were elected to positions similar to those they'd held in the Village.

On November 15th, the first load of equipment for the $1,000,000 water works had arrived, and work was started on a test well.

On December 13th, it was announced that 340 residents of the Stockton area would receive water service from the Fairfield Water Works.

Thus ended the year of triumph.

CHAPTER VI

Recapitulation

As we arrive at that part of history when Fairfield is about to embark on its venture as a full-fledged city, I reflect on the circumstances that brought us to this point.

The basic cause of the evolution was the continuing post-World War II demand for new housing, new living conditions, and land upon which to place those items.

The proximate cause was the desire to retain the *status quo*, in the desire of the residents to retain the Fairfield School system as nearly as possible the way it was. The school, in addition to being the lynch pin of the Township, was also the social center for the community.

Hamilton was confronted with the realization of its need to expand its border. The available home building space within its boundary had been reduced to just about zero. From Hamilton's point of view, the solution to the problem was simple: It would expand its borders in every possible direction, and obtain the real property necessary so as to provide the buildable land that was needed. Hamilton approached the solution in a straight-forward manner based on an apparently inbred notion that everyone should be so lucky as to be a part of Hamilton. To my recollection, all Hamilton officialdom believed this as an article of faith. Prior to publishing the Master Plan, there was no inquiry as to opinion of surrounding property owners, no public relations. It was just the Queen bestowing Knighthood on less-than-deserving recipients.

The master plan was the gasoline cast upon the embers of Fairfield's earlier interest in possible incorporation to preserve the life-style of the community.

The gasoline did not make what happened happen. It made what happened happen when it did. Resistance would have occurred whenever the plan appeared or whenever annexation threatened the Fairfield School system or the industrial base of Fairfield Township. None can say what the final result would have been, but it is certain that the resistance would have been there.

In his book, "Butler County in the 1900's", Hamilton historian James Blount, lists the ten major events that occurred in Butler County during the 20th century. One of these events is the formation of the City of Fairfield. It certainly was.

Had the City of Hamilton performed the ultimate in public relations, and had it coddled the residents of Fairfield Township to a copious degree, could they have annexed any significant part of Fairfield Township? I doubt it.

In any event, the creation of the City of Fairfield produced the most exciting demonstration of our courts, our laws, our Constitution in action that any county saw in the last half of the 20th century.

It made trial lawyers of Carl Kollstedt and me. As we became a City in 1955, and he and I reflected on the events, we determined that for 14 months beginning in early 1954, we had appeared at least once a week before either an administrative body, the Common Pleas Court, or the Court of Appeals.

It also made travelers of Helen and me, as we made many trips to Columbus and the State House seeking information and assistance. Treasurer Winifred Field also became knowledgeable about the then country roads to the Capitol. There were no freeways in 1955-56.

I wish I could live through the period again.

CHAPTER VII

City Life

As the new year 1956 began, the Council and Offices of the City were poised for action. They had been sworn in by Judge P.P. Boli and met January 9th to consider these matters on the agenda:

- To approve a budget in keeping with the estimated receipts of $70,000.00;
- To name a Civil Services Commission whose first duties would be to conduct examinations for a Chief of Police and a Fire Chief. The Police Chief would be a first and the Fire Chief would replace Jack McCormick who had moved to Florida;
- To establish a Planning Commission;
- To set new rules and regulations governing Council meetings and procedure;
- To know that the test well for the Fairfield Water Works had been completed.

This meeting was held in the Fire Department Firehouse after the trucks had been rolled out and folding chairs had been arranged to seat the public.

The City had no adequate place in which to meet. No police department, a barely adequate fire department. There were no administrative boards. No zoning ordinance, and insufficient monies to remedy these inadequacies.

All of this was occurring against a background where some of the comments were:

> "I'll tell you one thing. If things keep going the way they are, it's going to be impossible to buy a week's groceries for $20.00."
>
> "Have you seen the new cars coming out next year? It won't be long when $5,000.00 will only buy a used one."
>
> "Did you hear the post office is thinking about charging a dime just to mail a letter?"
>
> "If they raise the minimum wage to $1.00, nobody will be able to hire outside help at the store."
>
> "When I first started driving, who would have thought gas would someday cost 50 cents a gallon? Guess we'd be better off leaving the car in the garage."
>
> "Did you see where some baseball player just signed a contract for $75,000.00 a year just to play ball? It wouldn't surprise me if someday they'll be making more than the president."
>
> "It's too bad things are so tough nowadays. I see where a few married women are having to work to make ends meet."
>
> "It won't be long before young couples are going to have to hire someone to watch their kids so they can both work."
>
> "Next thing you know, the government will be paying us not to grow crops."
>
> "Thank goodness I won't live to see the day when the government takes half our income in taxes. I sometimes wonder if we are electing the best people to Congress."
>
> "Pretty soon you won't be able to buy a good 10 cent cigar."
>
> "I don't know about you, but if they raise the price of coffee to 15 cents, I'll just have to drink mine at home."

> *"No one can afford to be sick anymore. $35.00 a day in the hospital is too rich for my blood."*

Television was in its infancy. Black and white only; no color. Three channels.

Many houses did not have television sets. Almost no homes had more than one set, and it was usually mounted in a large cabinet. The cabinet encased a 12" picture tube. The whole family watched television together. The top-rated shows were *"I Love Lucy"* and *"$64,000 Question"*.

Our president was Dwight D. Eisenhower. His campaign buttons read: *"I Like Ike".* He was first elected in 1952, and would be re-elected in 1956. One of the major Congressional events of 1956 was the Federal Aid Highway Act, which was signed June 29th. It inaugurated the Interstate Highway System.

Automobile travel was slow compared to present standards. Travel from Fairfield to Cincinnati took one hour. You traveled either Route 127 (Mount Pleasant Pike) or Route 4 (Dixie Highway). You were continually passing through smaller communities, and stopping for traffic signals every few minutes.

A trip to Columbus was an all day affair. Leave early in the morning, conduct your business and return to Fairfield in early evening. If we perchance had a council meeting scheduled on a day we also had a Columbus trip, we would leave the door to our new home open and all the members would go in and start the meeting if we were not back from Columbus. This happened twice during Village days.

There were passenger trains, and the famed Baltimore and Ohio's Cincinnatian, one of the handsomest trains of the steam era, daily passed through Fairfield on its way from Cincinnati to Detroit and return. The Pennsylvania Railroad had daily service from Cincinnati to Chicago and return.

There was hourly bus service via Dixie Highway and Mount Pleasant Pike from Fairfield to Cincinnati. There was also service to Middletown and Oxford and points in between.

Fairfield was wide open space, dotted with small clusters of houses. There were no grocery stores as such. At Symmes Corner we had Mike Cepluch's delicatessen, and Mrs. Butterfield's living room to provide very basic grocery supplies. Kroger was the first large chain to come to Fairfield. In 1957, they opened a store in what would become the Hicks Manor Shopping Center.

There were no clothing or department stores in Fairfield. Shopping centers were in their infancy throughout the country. Serious shopping meant a trip to downtown Cincinnati. Men wore coats and hats, and women hats and white gloves on these occasions.

The favorite entertainment of most Fairfieldians was going to the movies. Tickets were less than $1.00, and color movies were just becoming common. The top picture of 1956 was *"Around the World in 80 Days"*. Top actor was Yul Brynner in *"The King and I"*; top actress Ingrid Bergman in *"Anastasia"*.

The top picture in 1957 was *"The Bridge Over The River Kwai"*. Top actor, Alec Guiness for his work in the *"Bridge"*, and actress Joanne Woodward in *"The Three Faces of Eve"*.

Recordings were big, and many people collected records. The industry had moved from 78's to 45's, and now 33-1/3's. It was yet the Swing Era, and the Big Bands. Tommy Dorsey, Benny Goodman, Duke Ellington, and Count Basie were the top bands. Frank Sinatra, Perry Como, Bing Crosby were top male vocalists. Patti Page, Jo Stafford, and Dinah Shore were the top female vocalists.

Many Fairfield people were baseball fans. In 1956, New York Yankees, American league defeated Brooklyn of the National league to win the World Series 4 games to 3. Yogi Berra, Yankees, and Roy Campanella, Dodgers, were the Most Valuable Players in their respective leagues.

In football, the New York Giants won the National Football League. There was no Super Bowl until 1967. Oklahoma was the National College Football Champions.

The one bright entertainment spot in Fairfield was Symmes Tavern. This historic tavern, owned and managed by Otto and Mrs. Keulthau, was known throughout the Tri-State area for its fine meals, European atmosphere, and superb beer. In a time when dining out was not the casual affair that it is today, Symmes Tavern was busy nightly with contented diners visiting Symmes Tavern after council meetings became routine and did much to insure unity of purpose for Village officers and Council members.

Symmes Tavern was purchased and handsomely remodeled by Bank One, and the old bar space houses the teller's counter. I've visited the Bank many times, but when I step up to the teller, may be it's just not the same.

When I view these events from my present-day perspective, I recall being in high school and seeing news reels of the soldiers marching in a Victory Parade at the end of World War I. This would have been 20 years after the war ended, and as they marched along in what seemed to be triple time because of the change in the speed the movie film had caused, they seemed unreal to me.

I hope that my effort here to allow you to see the ensuing events in the frame of the times will allow you to sense that all of the participants are very real, and that the events are truly historic.

Back to our lack of money. It didn't slow us down. We were not deterred. We pushed ahead as though we were the richest city in the world.

The most important project was the construction of the Fairfield Water Works and delivery system. With respect to this question, the *Journal News* reported on February 10th:

*As a community project, the Fairfield Civitan Club at
its regular meeting voted unanimously to assist in providing information regarding the greatly enlarged
Fairfield water system to all residents of the community.*

*Mayor Robert Wessel, in explaining the new citywide
water system said that at first only a limited area was to
be served. Now Fairfield Council has decided to serve the
whole city of Fairfield sanitary, softened water.*

*The new area to be served includes State Rte. 4 to the
Butler-Hamilton County line, Seward, Ross, Mack,
Gilmore, Winton, Mulhauser, and Stockton Rds., and
adjacent areas.*

One of Largest

*The Fairfield water system will be one of the largest, in
area, ever installed in entirety at one time, and will serve
some 1,600 users, providing added sanitary safety and
increased fire protection, said Mayor Wessel.*

By May 18th, work had begun on the Fairfield Water Plant. The estimated cost of the system was $1,500,000.00. By this time, a Civil Service
Commission had been appointed and they were working toward con-
ducting Civil Service examinations for the appointment of a Chief of
Police.

A Planning Commission had been appointed and was working
toward preparation of a comprehensive zoning ordinance.

The Civil Service Commission set the Police Chief exam for June 1st,
and on June 8th it was announced that Charles L. Hawkins was to be
appointed Fairfield's first Chief. He took office on July 1st, thus beginning what was to be a checkered career. However, he proved to be the
most popular police officer the City has thus far known.

On June 10th, the Ground Breaking Ceremony for the Municipal Water System was held at the well site at McCormick Lane and River Road. It was a most impressive ceremony.

The new plant being constructed by the Coleman-Trainor Company at a cost of in excess of $1,000,000.00 would initially serve more than 2000 households and have a one million gallon per day capacity. The system could provide ample water for 35,000 persons, and the plant would have capacity to treat water for up to 12,000 persons.

On June 19th, Warren Harding, Mrs. Lewis Burkett, and Mrs. George Zimmers, representing the Fairfield Resident's Committee, presented the first copy of the City of Fairfield Directory, which had been compiled and published by the Resident's Committee.

The Civil Service Commission set August 7th as the date on which examinations would be held for police patrolmen. The exams were held, successful applicants named, and appointments made. By Fairfield's one year anniversary, there was a five-man force in place and on the job. Charles Hawkins was the Chief, and James Bannon, Glenn Weber, James Eve and James Walsh were the patrolmen. James Walsh moved onward and upward as he became in succession a lawyer, judge of the Fairfield Municipal Court, and is presently a judge for the 12th District Court of Appeals for Fairfield.

Relations with Hamilton became front and center in September. The widow of Darrell E. Joyce devised a 250-acre tract of land to the City of Hamilton, specifying that it had be developed for public purposes within three years. If not so developed, the land was to be sold and the proceeds given to the Salvation Army. The problem was the land is situated in the City of Fairfield.

This resulted in a joint meeting between the officers and councilmen of the cities to resolve the dilemma. At the meeting, the position of Hamilton was that they wanted to annex the property. The position of Fairfield was clear and adamant: No annexation.

After many letters, more meetings, and great posturing on both sides, the matter was resolved on the following terms:

(1)   That Fairfield grant Hamilton utility easements to the park;

(2)   That egress and ingress to the area be provided;

(3)   That Hamilton be permitted to give police protection; and,

(4)   Fire protection to the area.

The development of Joyce Park proceeded under these terms and continues on this basis today. It continues to be a huge success.

The Planning Committee of Council and the Planning Commission continued work on completing a comprehensive zoning ordinance. By November 19th, work had progressed to the point of completion and public hearings would be held early in the New Year.

The City accepted the newly completed water plant on December 26th, and as the New Year was on the horizon, two thousand customers began the process of tapping into the system.

The Mayor's Court had been in operation almost a full year, and over 500 cases had been heard.

I will never forget the first case I heard in Mayor's Court.

I need to set the scene: At the time, the Village of Fairfield had no police department, less than rudimentary court facilities, and no clerk. We depended on the Ohio State Highway Patrol and Fairfield Township Constables to enforce the law.

On this fateful Saturday afternoon, a State Trooper came to my home and said that he had arrested a speeder, and could he bring him to Mayor's Court.

I was excited and slightly apprehensive since I was pristine at being a judge.

I was, however, a lawyer of four years experience, although my practice was small.

So, it was off to the firehouse to hear that first case. As I took my seat at one of the Formica tables my father-in-law had provided and confronted the miscreant seated on the back of a fire engine, my enthusiasm greatly waned. The person seated on the fire engine was Anthony Becker, owner and operator of the Mount Pleasant Bakery, sterling among my then meager list of clients.

He pled guilty. I fined him fifty dollars plus costs, and returned home in much subdued spirits. I thought about Sherman and what war is.

The story has a happy outcome. Anthony Becker remained a sterling client and, to this day, I still have the honor of being his counsel.

The Mayor's Court was a fascinating place to watch misdemeanor cases unfold. My most memorable case occurred just before Christmas. A black man of huge proportions had been cited for speeding 70 m.p.h. in a 35 m.p.h. zone.

After the facts had been related and, feeling in the Christmas spirit, I said to the defendant: *"If you were sitting where I'm sitting, and I were sitting where you're sitting, what would you say?"*

He said, *"Man, I'd look at you and say, there is a guy who deserves a break."*

I said to him, *"How about a $50.00 fine, and the court costs?"*

He said, *"Man! You don't call that no break!"*

I suspended the fine.

The newly formed Fairfield Chamber of Commerce sponsored the dinner celebrating the first anniversary of the City. It was titled: "Preview of the Future".

On that occasion, writing for the *Cincinnati Post*, Elsa Simpson, Butler County reporter for the *Post*, wrote:

> **FAIRFIELD, Oct. 27—Like an eager youngster blowing out the candles on a cake with dreams of glorious**

tomorrows, the City of Fairfield is in a "birthday" mood today.

She is one year old…and a lot of skeptics said she would never make it.

Tonight at a banquet in the Fairfield school there will be a birthday celebration for a city, with each of more than 6000 citizens as proud as parents. Most of them have had a hand in the making of this city and they and generations to come will benefit by the courage of its officials who have seen that Fairfield has many new things during its first and probably most difficult year.

The committee for the event included the Chamber of Commerce officers and some representative citizens. At the final meeting with Chamber officers were Custer Reynolds, master of the ceremonies and principal of Fairfield school; Dr. Arthur Schalk, president of the Resident's Association and retired medical man; Harold Follmer, industrial chairman of the Chamber and a member of the board of directors; and Kenneth Webb, chairman of the Fairfield Boy Scouts. Others have had a hand in plans too.

They will celebrate today, the new accomplishments of the new city.

First and foremost they have a water works. Water was pumped through the lines first on October 15, and some 1,800 homes are now tapping in for service. The plant built at a cost of $1,350,000 by the Coleman-Trainor Co., of Huntington, West Va. is located on E. River Rd. Builders say it is designed for expansion expected in Fairfield.

Also new in Fairfield is the Police Department, headed by Chief Charles Hawkins; a new Chamber of

Commerce, headed by O.J. Chiappe; a brand new weekly newspaper, the "Fairfield Echo" put out by Charles T. Logsdon, a 21-year old Miami University senior; some new fire equipment for Chief Harmon Moss and his volunteers, and many other things, all aimed at insuring the future.

In the business way there are two new sports centers, plans for a large office building, and plans for a golf course.

A fitting title for the birthday celebration is "Preview of the Future", and it looks like a bright one for Fairfield.

She also had occasion to interview me on that same date, after which she wrote the following article:

FAIRFIELD, Oct 27—A bright future for a city he has headed since it became a village is seen by Mayor Robert F. Wessel.

The young attorney says his terms of office have been "interesting, delightful and lots of work."

"I think the future of Fairfield has been assured by the installation of the Municipal Water Works, and the installation of gas mains by the Cincinnati Gas and Electric company," he said.

"I believe Fairfield is on the brink of vast and diversified industrial development along the major railroads passing through.

"In the interest of a rapid future development it is the opinion of Council and the officials of the city of Fairfield that it is necessary that additional financing for municipal affairs be provided," he said. "It is imperative voters of Fairfield support the request for a two mill levy on Nov. 6.

"This will allow more rapid and better repair of streets and highway development, and an expansion of dumping facilities for disposal of garbage. These funds also will provide for expansion and development of fire services and additional police protection in the modernization of radio and police department facilities."

The two-mill levy that the city had placed on the ballot to acquire funds for general operation of the City failed at the November 6th election.

As the year waned, the most critical item remaining before Council concerned the rights of the homeowners in Hicks Manor Subdivision.

On December 17th, several residents of Hicks Manor Subdivision attended the caucus meeting of the Fairfield City Council, and asked Council not to service that area with water from the new $1,500,000 water plant until a satisfactory settlement has been reached on reimbursement to the residents for the installation of water lines.

Councilmen William Holden, Jack Daughterty and Francis Miller were appointed by Council President Larry Lloyd to meet with a three-man committee of residents to discuss equitable settlement.

The homes in that subdivision were then receiving water from the City of Hamilton through water lines installed by the sub-divider, and paid for by the residents through the purchase of their homes.

The Fairfield Council had previously announced that water from the new plant would be sent through those pipes on or about January 1, 1957, and that Hicks Manor residents would pay the same water rates as other residents in the City. The minimum water rate in Fairfield was $4.25 for 3,000 gallons of water a month, and this charge included about $3 toward paying off the cost of constructing the new water plant.

Homeowners in the subdivision claimed they had already paid for the installation of their lines (before the city was incorporated) when purchasing their homes, and did not feel that they should have to pay the existing Fairfield water rates and part of the installation costs of residents in other area of the City.

I explained that since the City of Fairfield was responsible for the servicing of any and all broken water lines in the subdivision, and the repair of streets damaged by repairing such lines, the city is desirous of taking over the water lines in the area.

I said that the lines, by law, became the property of the City of Fairfield when the municipality was formed, and that the Council has a legal right to supply water for these lines.

A majority of members of Council appeared to be interested in making some sort of financial settlement with the residents, but the latter group presented no specific requests.

After lengthy discussion, the upshot of the matter was a resolution of Council that a three-member committee of Council and a three-member committee of Hicks Manor residents meet to see if the matter could be amicably resolved. A February 1, 1957, deadline was set as a time when Fairfield would begin furnishing water to Hicks Manor residents.

Mrs. Esther Benzing, 3051 Mack Road, asked Council to consider the use of volunteer police officers so as to have two patrolmen in the cruisers at all times. She cited a recent incident in the city where one officer was responsible for three law violators.

A Finance Committee report showed the city had a surplus of funds of $23,940 at the end of that current year. Council proposed spending this surplus as follows:

Dump Truck	$ 4,000.00
Road Roller	$ 6,000.00
Additional office space for city personnel	$10,000.00
Road Grader	$ 4,000.00

Thus a busy and tempestuous year ended.

CHAPTER VIII

The End of the Beginning

There was not much difference between old year's end and new year's beginning.

Council voted to place a two-mill levy on the ballot, and to hold a special election on the question in early Spring.

Negotiations between the Council Committee and the Hicks Manor Committee continued, and the deadline for settlement of the question was extended to April 1st.

City Council in March approved an appropriation ordinance showing appropriations totaling $144,362 for the fiscal year 1957. This total was the entire amount of anticipated funds the City would receive from all sources during the year. It made painfully obvious the need for additional funding.

On March 11th, the first reading of the comprehensive zoning ordinance was read after several amendments had been made. The second reading was approved on March 25th, and the third and final reading was approved and the Zoning Ordinance adopted on April 8th.

At the March 25th meeting, Council approved a resolution making the chrysanthemum the City Flower. What transpired thereafter when a resident asked the Council to consider a City Motto was reported in the *Journal-News* as follows:

> *At its regular meeting Monday night, Fairfield*
> *Council approved the recommendation of the Fair*

Haven Garden Club "that the chrysanthemum be named as the city flower."

Following this approval, a resident asked the Council to also consider a motto for the city. The seven-member Council, faced with many serious problems, was silent for a few moments.

Then, Mayor Robert Wessel spoke: "Mr. Chairman, I have always liked the slogan "When in doubt, punt."

The resulting hilarity postponed any further consideration of a city motto.

On Sunday, June 16th, the Fairfield Water Works was dedicated. Sponsored by the Fairfield Residents Association, it was a gala affair.

The program called for Robert Swain, then President of the Fairfield Residents Association and I to arrive at the dedication ceremony by helicopter. The plan was that Swain and I were to board the helicopter in John Slade's open field at the southwest corner of Symmes Road and Route 4, and be airlifted across the City to the Water Works plant where the dedication ceremony was to transpire. Helen drove me to the boarding spot, and Swain and I jumped aboard and were quickly whisked across the City to the ceremonial site. The helicopter ride was a first for me, and was an awe-inspiring experience. The cockpit of the helicopter was open and the passengers were restrained by a web lap belt, which crossed the laps of both passengers. The ride provided a fascinating view of the City, and a visual reaffirmation of its size and scope.

Upon arrival, the program was:

12:00-	*Presentation of Colors* *—Boy Scouts*
1:30-	*Arrival of Mayor Robert Wessel and Res. Assoc. Pres. Robert Swain by Helicopter*
2:00-	*Official Dedication of Water Works.*
2:30-	*Music—-Fairfield H.S. Band.*

| 4:00- | Retiring the Colors | —Boy Scouts |

| 12:00-4:00 | Conducted Tours |
| 1:30-4:30 | Helicopter Rides. |

Refreshments by the Boy Scouts
GIFTS

The program contained the following facts about the water system:

Cost of Plant $1,525,00
Subscribers 1400
Capacity ....(2 Wells) 1000 gal. a minute
Expansion ....6X present usage
Amount of Mains ....36 miles of pipes
Capacity of Tanks ....750,000 gal.
Capacity of Mains ....1,000,000 gal.
Water Pumped-day average ....225,000 gal.
Used-Family-day average..............................120 gal.
Used-Person-day average....................................30 gal.

WMOH broadcast the proceedings.

Helen was on the scene, as was our good friend, Councilman Ellis Muskopf. After some discussion, they decided to take the $5.00 helicopter spin offered to everyone there. They were both awe-struck, as was I, at the experience.

July 4, 1957, was on a Thursday. The City of Fairfield was in the midst of completing the installation of its waterworks. Construction was well underway, every street had been cut, water lines installed and then back-filled and, as the holiday dawned, almost every driveway in Fairfield had been cut to permit the water service lines to be installed.

The cuts had been back-filled with gravel to give residents access to their property.

The contractor who was installing the water lines decided that the holiday was a great chance for a long weekend. His employees would work on Wednesday and then not return until the following Monday. They elected one hapless soul to remain with his truck in case there was an emergency. The contractor's gang were all from West Virginia and, by the time they had cleared Cincinnati, it began to rain in our fair city.

The rain continued all night on July 3rd, and it was still raining very hard by noon time on July 4th. Had there been such bulletins in those days, flood warnings would have been filling the air waves throughout the city.

By this time, an interesting phenomenon had occurred. Every back-filled driveway in Fairfield had sunk at least a foot, making it impossible for the residents to leave or enter their property.

As the complaints of the citizens intent on holiday merry-making clogged our phone line, Helen and I quickly discovered that it was not going to be a fun day to be Mayor-City Manager. We had to solve the problem.

We called the lone employee of the contractor; we called our ever-reliable Safety-Service Director, Paul Conrad, who brought the one and only Fairfield dump truck, and I borrowed my father-in-law's pickup truck and we set out to backfill driveways.

Helen answered the telephone, while our three-man force went from driveway to driveway rescuing the holiday for our patriotic citizens. By the time evening had come, we had abandoned early our plans to join friends for a picnic celebration.

Dusk had fallen when the phone rang one more time. The caller said that he had a driveway problem. I apologized, and said that I thought we had backfilled every Fairfield driveway. He said we had backfilled his driveway, but the gravel was too deep and it was hard to get in or out.

I told him that they made an instrument to solve the problem. He said, "What?"

I told him it was a shovel.

Thus ended the day.

On May 7th, Fairfield voters defeated the proposed 5-mill levy for the General Fund. This drastically reduced our street repair program.

Also on May 7th, Council authorized new Water Works bonds totaling $50,000—of which $33,000 was paid to the Hick's Manor residents in compensation for their water lines.

On July 5th, Chief of Police Charles Hawkins resigned after serious turmoil throughout the city concerning a carnival he had improvidently allowed to do business in the City. After Civil Service exams had been conducted, Sam Bowling was appointed Chief of Police in August.

My term was winding down, and 1957 was a municipal election year. I felt that in order to see the City firmly implanted and set, I should seek another term of office.

William O. Holden, who had been an unsuccessful candidate for Mayor at the first Village of Fairfield election and who was then a member of Fairfield Council, had a different idea. He ran as my opponent, campaigned vigorously and snidely.

When the votes were counted, he won the election.

The vote count was Holden: 1,237; and Wessel: 789.

Helen said, "Look at it this way: How would you feel if you were looking forward to two more years of being mayor?"

She was right, of course. Being mayor provoked ambivalent feelings. On the one hand, it was a great honor, and being mayor filled you with pride. On the other hand, it was, at the time, a position of unremitting responsibility. The mayor was involved in every meeting, and many situations when he was on his own. It seemed that every decision created a friend and many times a foe.

In the same issue of the *Fairfield Chronicle* that announced my defeat, there was an architect's sketch showing the office building which Champion Paper and Fibre Company was going to build in the City of Fairfield. I was a lame duck mayor for two more months.

When you drive north on Neilan Boulevard in the City of Hamilton, and are approaching Knightsbridge Drive, if you look to the right you can't miss the imposing complex that was Champion International. If you are in a reflective mood, you might ponder the question of how such an unusual looking main building happened to be on this site.

The story is an interesting one, and probably has been long forgotten over the forty-four years that have passed since it all began. The year was 1957, and the animosity between the City of Hamilton and the City of Fairfield, although subdued, could hardly have been classified as reaching the merely smoldering stage.

During the course of the year, Champion International (then Champion Paper and Fibre Company) had taken an option on the Story farm, which was situated in the City of Fairfield, and began at the intersection of Nilles Road and Mt. Pleasant Avenue on the southeast corner. The farm extended to the south and to the east. To the south, it reached a point where it nestled under the brow of a hill. It was, and is, a truly beautiful site.

From the beginning of the year, it was an open secret that Champion International had taken an option on the property, and was planning to use it as a site for new corporate headquarters.

We move forward in time to early December, 1957. Many earth-shattering events had occurred during the course of the year, the most important as far as I was concerned was the fact that it was an election year, and my efforts to be re-elected as mayor of the City had been thwarted.

At any rate, I was sitting in my office on this day, musing to myself about the general state of affairs, and thinking it would be good if we could nail down a commitment from Champion to located in Fairfield.

With this in mind, I called Champion and asked to speak to Herbert Randall who was, at that time, the head of everything at Champion. After a short delay, he was on the line and I got to make my pitch.

"Mr. Randall," I said, "I am Bob Wessel, the Mayor of Fairfield. The reason for my call is to see if the City of Fairfield can be of any help in your consideration of Fairfield as a place to locate your new corporate headquarters."

"We can't locate in Fairfield, because we need a good water supply, and there isn't any such thing to be had in Fairfield," he said.

"Mr. Randall, there is a 16 inch water line at the border of the property, right in the middle of Nilles Road," I said. "Is there anything else that Champion needs that we might provide?"

"The only other thing that you could provide to insure that Champion would accept this location is a Hamilton, Ohio postmark," he said.

"I'm sorry, Mr. Randall, but that's one thing I just can't do for you," I told him.

"In that case, Champion won't be coming," he retorted.

Thus ended my one and only discussion with Champion International about becoming a corporate citizen of Fairfield. For several days thereafter, I really didn't believe that Champion would forsake the picturesque and tree-shrouded beauty of the Fairfield site to located on the site of a former landfill in the City of Hamilton. Shortly hence, I left office and in the Spring of 1958, when the landscaping began on the old dump site, I became a believer.

The irony of it all from the vantage point of history is that, despite all of the efforts of John Slade and many other Fairfield boosters, Fairfield did not then and has not now persuaded the United States Post Office to make Fairfield a post office of its own. We continue to be a branch of the Hamilton Post Office.

So Champion could have come to Opportunity City, and basked in the beauty of their selected site. They could have retained their

Hamilton, Ohio postmark and enjoyed the friendly people who reside and work in Fairfield.

For a short time, there was disappointment in our City, but then other projects and ventures presented themselves and the memory of what might have been faded and, by this time, some 46 years later, only a few remember the saga of the City of Fairfield and Champion International.

In 1963, when Ed Bartels was the Mayor of our fair city, it became very apparent that a growing city needed better facilities in which to conduct municipal affairs. By some special magic, the City of Fairfield acquired a portion of the Story Farm and, after due passage of time, what should appear nestled under the brow of the hill on the Story Farm, but the present Fairfield Municipal Building. It was, and is, a beautiful site. To my great pleasure and satisfaction, the street that passes the city building was named Wessel Drive at Mr. Bartel's suggestion with the Council's approval.

At the November election, the Fairfield voters again defeated a 2-mill General Operating levy.

On Monday, December 23rd, I attended my final meeting as Mayor. I made my final yearly report, which the *Fairfield Chronicle* reported as follows:

> *"The Fairfield City Council met in regular session on Monday evening at 8 p.m. at the City Fire House, Pleasant Avenue.*
>
> *Mayor Robert Wessel gave the annual report to Council as it is the duty of the Mayor to report at each year's end concerning the activities and file a report concerning the status of the City during the period, said Mayor Wessel.*
>
> *There were many innovations for the City of Fairfield during the year of 1957. The primary one being the*

increased activity in an effort to bring Fairfield streets to an acceptable condition. A road grader-roller and an additional truck was provided for street repair. A great deal of street repair was accomplished for the amount of money, approximately $30,000.00, which was spent for this purpose. Mayor Wessel also said the streets are not in first class condition, but they are in better condition than they have been at any time over the past five years. Lack of funds was the main reason for no major repairs, and the same situation will apply next year unless some means are found to augment the present income of the City.

The year 1957, according to Mayor Wessel's report, also saw our Fairfield Municipal Water Works brought to completion and placed in operation, the number of customers for water, when first placed in operation, was 1251 and during the year this number has grown to approximately 1600 customers. Some time during the year it will be necessary to pick up the $225,000.00 General Obligation Note which is now outstanding, but since it is anticipated that the first payment will not be due until 1960, revenues of the system will be sufficient to pay this obligation, as well as the First Mortgage Revenue bonds which were issued last year.

The annual report also lists the Hicks Manor water lines as becoming a part of the Fairfield system and was a great demonstration of cooperation between citizens and government, and resulted in fair and equitable settlement for all parties.

Another project was the Planning Commission and Council completing the comprehensive zoning ordinance, going from a no zoning whatsoever to a complete type of zoning ordinance.

Fairfield had been fortunate in maintaining a high level of building, when most of the nation has experienced a slump in this field. Nearly 170 new units were under construction in 1957. The Council Committee for Industrial Development and the Chamber of Commerce have worked to bring about industrial development in the community.

Mayor Wessel stated that since Chief Bowling of the Fairfield Police Department has recently reported on the last quarter activity, he would not review in detail these activities. But he praised Chief Bowling and the police officers for a fine job of protection for the citizens of Fairfield, considering the large area which must be policed with the minimum number of police officers.

The Mayor's Court disclosed that there were a total of 498 cases heard during 1957, in comparison with a total of 720 cases in 1956. Much of this number of cases was accounted for by the decrease in State Patrol activity in and around the area, and to the fact that there were very few state cases heard by the Mayor's Court this year. Total receipt from fines, costs, and permits by the Mayor during this period were $11,810.74. This was comprised of ordinance fines, costs and permits in the sum of $11,280.79, which have been paid into the Municipal Treasury. There will be a slight increase because of three outstanding cases. $140.00 was paid to the Treasurer of Butler County in State Cases, and a total of $168.95 was paid to the State Treasurer for state highway arrests. $40.00 was paid into the Police Pension Fund. The report *continues: During 1957 the Police Pension and Retirement Board was established.*

During 1957 the Civil Service Commission continued to operate and has gone from a humble beginning to a fully proficient Civil Service Commission. Mayor Wessel said in completing his report, that he was completing one full term as Mayor of the City of Fairfield and one term as Mayor of the Village of Fairfield, and he wished to express his deep appreciation to the people of the City for, according to him, the honor of serving as their Mayor. He also expressed his gratitude to Walter DeLano, Tom Jacobi and Joe Montaine for the fine work on the Planning Commission; to John Francis, John Tallen and Roland Ream for their good work on the Civil Service Commission, and thanks to Paul Conrad, Director of Public Service and Safety, for his untiring efforts which have been legion on the part of the City of Fairfield, Ohio. Also thanks to Chief of Police Bowling and the officers of the Fairfield Fire Department, which have also been legion. Also thanks to Ben Groh who has rendered invaluable assistance in the operation of the Mayor's Court in the City of Fairfield."

Thus, the beginning ended.

EPILOGUE

As the new year dawned, I was convinced that the City would disintegrate in my absence. But to my great surprise, the new slate of officers struggled on not seeming to notice that I wasn't there.

I remembered a conversation I had with my attorney friend, Richard Koehler, who would later serve a distinguished career as judge of the 12th District Court of Appeals, which district includes Butler County. We were in attendance at the dedication of the Union Hall for Local 233, UAW AFL-CIO, on Sunday, September 29, 1957. Local 233 was the chapter that represented the Fisher Body employees and the Union had constructed a fine building to service its employees. I was a speaker and the *Fairfield Chronicle* reported on this event as follows:

> *Robert F. Wessel, Mayor of Fairfield City, expressed the good wishes of the city council and executive officials and how proud we are to have this fine building in our city. Said Mayor Wessel, "We know the city, the new building and the union can prosper and grow together."*

When the ceremony had ended, Dick and I were talking when a union member came up, shook my hand, congratulated me on my speech, and said, "I know you're running for reelection. Do you have any cards with you? I really want to help you get elected." He left, and as he walked away, Dick said, "Put him down as doubtful."

After the November 1957 election results were known, I thought Dick indeed was prophetic.

I remained totally interested in the continuing progress of the City, but from a distance.

In May 1960, I was elected to a commission to frame a charter for the City, and after a year's effort, we submitted a proposed charter to the voters, which was defeated. There was not another attempt to frame a charter until 1978, which effort resulted in the adoption of a charter by the voters in 1979. The City still operates under this City Manager form of government today.

In 1966, I ran unopposed for the position of City Solicitor-Law Director of Fairfield. I was elected and, for the next ten years, was the legal advisor to the City. Between 1960-1966, I had served on the Planning Commission and the Board of Zoning Appeals.

At the time my term as Solicitor ended, the City was involved in a case brought against it by Towne Properties. The suit arose out of an ordinance establishing a $50.00 tax on each newly constructed single family and multiple residential unit to be used for recreational purposes in the City.

Towne Properties had paid the tax, amounting to $9,700.00 under protest, and had sued the City claiming the tax to be unconstitutional.

On September 17, 1975, Judge Fred B. Cramer of the Butler County Common Pleas Court found the tax to be unconstitutional. We had appealed the decision to the First District Court of Appeals.

Fred B. Cramer was a giant in the long annals of Butler County Common Pleas Judges. He was short in stature and acerbic of wit. He served 34 years on the Common Pleas bench, longer than any other person thus far.

Shortly after my term as mayor ended, I was attorney for the plaintiff in a two-day jury trial in Judge Cramer's Courtroom. The jury was deliberating, and Judge Cramer, the attorney for the defendant, and I were sitting in his office awaiting a verdict.

Apropos of nothing, I said, "It's a sad day for me."

Judge Cramer said, "Why?"

"Because my father-in-law is selling his pick-up truck."

"Why is that making you sad? What did you want?"

I said, "I wanted him to give it to me."

Judge Cramer asked, "What would you do with it?"

"I'd put a sign on the door: Robert F. Wessel, Lawyer. Also light hauling."

Judge Cramer reflected a moment. Then, true to his reputation said, "Put the 'light hauling' first."

My term was ending, and the City was not confident of the validity of the tax. Since I had spent much effort in drafting the ordinance so as to assure its validity, I asked the counsel for authority to pursue the appeal without fee and at my cost. They agreed.

The Court of Appeals affirmed the trial court.

I appealed the Supreme Court of Ohio, which on June 29, 1977 over-ruled the lower courts and found the tax to be valid and constitutional.

The tax has been imposed by the city to the present date. It has pro-duced over $1,000,000.00 in revenues for recreational purposes. I am totally pleased with this outcome.

Each five years, starting with the fifth, there was a dinner honoring the birth of the City, and I was honored to be recognized and to speak as the First Mayor. These yearly events reached their apex in 1991, when the City celebrated for a week honoring the 40th anniversary of the City. There were concerts, picnics, city tours, and historical exhibits. The climax was a banquet held at Receptions attended by 350 people. I was the honored speaker. It was a great day.

In 1988, Helen and I became involved in the effort to save and restore what is now known as the Elisha Morgan Farm Mansion, circa 1817. During this year, we had remodeled and expanded our home. Ann Antenen, our friend and a noted restoration architect, had been in charge of the remodeling. At some point in the work, she mentioned the farmhouse situated on the land in the Gilbert Farms Park. This park had been acquired by the City from the Gilbert family in 1979. She was part of a group of interested citizens who wished to restore the property and use it as a Fairfield museum. She wanted us to join the group.

We were not unfamiliar with what then was known as the Gilbert House, but we had not been in the house since the City had acquired it. We agreed to look, which we did.

What we saw was a totally uninspiring sight. The building was in a rundown, dilapidated condition. Windows were missing. The City had permitted the Fairfield Athletic Association to use the home as a Halloween haunted house, and they had painted the entire interior black. Vandals had burned the mantel of one of the fireplaces. Graffiti was rampant. In spite of this gloomy appraisal, Ann convinced us that the building was structurally sound, and that much of the woodwork, mantels, and floor could be restored. She pointed out that it was about the oldest building in Fairfield, that, if properly restored, it would be a wonderful Fairfield asset. We agreed to join the group, and give it a try.

The situation was desperate, in that the City had already appropriated funds to have the structure demolished. The group appeared at the next Council meeting and asked Council to give us a chance to raise the funds and restore the building. The upshot was they deferred any action on razing the building for thirty days, and told us to see what funds we could raise and report back. It was the end of November, and Christmas was in the offing, not a good fund-raising time.

Nonetheless, after thirty days, we made the report. We had raised $6,000.00. It wasn't much when compared to the estimated cost of restoration, but it was more than all the previous fund raisers had raised over ten years. Council deferred the razing and elected to study the matter. Since no definite date was deferred to, we were forced to attend every Council meeting until some final decision was made.

As we lingered in limbo, we continued our fund raising efforts. We also enlisted the assistance of Bruce Goetzman, a noted restoration architect and professor at the University of Cincinnati. He agreed to meet with the group in the cafeteria of the high school one evening, and was greatly impressed with the number of cars in the parking lot. He met our group of seven people in the cafeteria, and discovered that there was a basketball game going on the gym.

Bruce agreed to assist us in our quest, and his joining proved to be a vital cog in the eventual successful restoration of the manse. He agreed to do a feasibility study as to the restoration, which he did. He found the restoration to be feasible.

On January 12, 1989, Council appointed a Museum Advisory Board to study the need for and make a recommendation of location for a Fairfield museum. The Board met each month until September 12, 1989, when it found a need for a museum and recommended Gilbert House for that purpose.

During this period, research with reference to the origin of the house was made. The first construction of the house was done by Elisha Morgan about 1817 A.D. At the same time, fund raising was proceeding. In order to spur the fund raising, and to give an historical aspect to the restoration, the official name of the group was made the Elisha Morgan Farm Mansion, Inc. It informally became known as the Friends of Elisha Morgan.

Time marched on. The City turned the house over to our group. We cleaned, promoted, raised money and sought any means to give the project impetus. By 1991, we had increased our funds to $11,000.00. We made application to the Ohio Arts Council for a matching grant to have work drawings and specifications completed. We were successful. Bruce Goetzman was engaged and completed the plans by early 1992.

Over the ensuing two years, we worked to raise funds. We held Garden Tours, meetings, sales, but made little progress toward restoration. In 1994, the City came to our aid and secured a Federal Block Grant of $120,400.00 to complete the exterior restoration of the house. The work was done under the supervision of Bruce Goetzman and completed in mid-1995.

The exterior restoration was wonderful, but nothing further could be accomplished until 1997, when the City obtained another matching grant and appropriated additional General Fund monies—in total $374,000—to complete the interior restoration. Cheryl Hilbert, Fairfield City Manager during these times deserves special credit for efforts as a stalwart friend of Elisha Morgan.

The interior restoration of the building was complete by May 23, 1998, when a gala pre-dedication dinner and program were held on site. The formal dedication was held on Sunday, May 26, 1998.

Since its dedication, the house has been the social crown jewel of the City. It has hosted many wedding receptions, parties, cultural programs and meetings. It was cited by the Cincinnati Preservation Association, and is listed in the National Register of Historic Places.

The list of persons who have been Friends to Elisha Morgan over the years would be long and impressive. Some important contributors would be missed. The present members are: Robert (President) and Helen Wessel; Jim and Karen Schwartz, Ann Antenen, Millie Suerman, Judy Dirksen, Dan Scofield, Theresa Durbin, Tom Jenkins, Linda Fitzgerald, Lori Simpson, and Tarana Ervin.

Over these intervening years, the City has seen expansion and growth that defies belief. The U.S. Census numbers are astounding:

October 20, 1957	6,202
Census 1960	9,734
Census 1970	15,342
Census 1980	30,777
Census 1990	39,709
Census 2000	42,907

After a great deal of thought and a comprehensive review of the events of the past 46 years, I conclude that the most important events leading to growth was the enactment of the City Income Tax on October 1, 1959.

During the first five years of municipal life, Fairfield struggled and improvised to do the basic government duties that are required of cities. Our police force was too small for our large area. We were hard pressed to maintain our roads. We had no other paid staff or workers.

The subject of enacting an income tax had been broached on numerous occasions, but was rejected in order to fulfill the pre-incorporation assurance that becoming a city would not bring about a rise in taxes.

An equally important reason for not acting was the fact that the City of Hamilton had no income tax.

The City of Hamilton depended for its general revenue on a general utility tax, that is, a tax on all of its utility services—water, gas and electricity—which then went into its general fund to support police, fire, street, and other ordinary functions of city government.

Fate was about to intervene.

The City of Franklin, Ohio had a similar utility tax and, in that city, a taxpayer filed suit against the city alleging that this general utility tax was unconstitutional because it did not distribute the tax burden equally against all citizens. Hamilton joined in the suit with Franklin.

The general utility tax was declared unconstitutional in the Fall of 1959. Hamilton enacted an income tax. This was sufficient impetus for the City of Fairfield to do the same.

The City of Fairfield lost its Talented Amateur status, and gradually moved to that of Competent and Professional. Our population in 1960 was 9,734. It had doubled by 1970, and almost doubled again in 1980 to 30,777. By 2000, it was 42,907.

Obviously, the two most significant events of the period that allowed Fairfield to truly become a city was the completion of a comprehensive water delivery system on June 16, 1957, and the opening of the Fairfield

Sanitary Sewer system on October 22, 1967. Without either of them, we would be a city in name only. Even a casual observer would select these events as being most significant and no further discussion is required.

On par with these events and of equal importance, was the adoption of the City Charter on June 5, 1979. This instrument provided a radical change in our form of government. It gave new momentum to our City which, after 22 years of existence, was starting to lag. It provided for top-drawer efficiency in administrative management. It enhanced the growth and development of our city. It provided for a city manager form of government that has well-served us over the years.

In retrospect, the founders of the City can bask in the realization that two of their goals were achieved:

1.   *The Fairfield City School system is alive and well; and,*
2.   *Fairfield Municipal self-government is thriving.*

A thriving, bustling community has supplanted the third goal for a quiet, peaceful suburban government. The founders would be happy about that.

As the city celebrated its first anniversary, John Slade said: "*Time passes in the Fairfield country, the older residents will have their shining memories, the new settlers will inevitably add vigor and vision. New obligations and responsibilities will arise. In its first century and a half, Fairfield has fulfilled its period of* Pioneer of the Past. *Time to come will provide* The Avenue of the Future.

As Fairfield looks toward its golden anniversary, the Avenue of the Future is a shining path.

In my address at the 40th anniversary, a part of what I said was:

> "*I'd like to tell you some of the exciting and humorous experiences that I encountered as mayor of Fairfield. There isn't enough time. I stand here as representative of a small group of Fairfield citizens who have experienced democracy*

and self-government at the root. Members of the Fairfield Residents Association were patriots. The first council of both the Village and City of Fairfield were blue ribbon.

In the early days, Helen was City Hall. She was secretary, Public Relations Director, and trouble-shooter. She was also grass cutter, leaf raker, and gardener, while I was engaged in affairs of state.

"Two periods of my life stand out above all the rest. The first was my service with the 908th Field Artillery during World War II; the second was my tenure as mayor of the City of Fairfield, Ohio. In both cases, the determination and singleness of purpose was the epitome of human endeavor.

"Finally, I commend the 40th Anniversary Committee who have worked long and hard to make the celebration a success. No city ever had a better 40th birthday.

"At the height of the Korean War, President Truman fired General McArthur. General McArthur, great as he was, was a consummate ham. He journeyed to the plains of West Point to deliver his farewell to the troops with tears welling in his eyes. In closing, he said "old soldiers never die, they just fade away."

"I paraphrase: Old lawyers never die, and they don't fade away. I look forward with gusto to the next decade and plan to see you all at the 50th anniversary, October 20, 2005."

What I said then still prevails. I am awaiting with patient anticipation to see what the Golden Anniversary will disclose.

Thus my tale is told.

Robert F. Wessel
December 2001

ABOUT THE AUTHOR

The author is a Butler County, Ohio native, and has practiced law in this area for more than 50 years. He is a World War II veteran, having served with the 83rd Infantry Division for 38 months, twenty months in the European Theatre.

He was one of the Founders of the City of Fairfield, and served as the First Mayor of both the Village of Fairfield and the City of Fairfield. He also served 10 years as Solicitor-Law Director from 1966-1976.

He and his wife, Helen, have been Fairfield residents for 50 years, and both were instrumental in the preservation and restoration of the Elisha Morgan Farm Mansion in the City.

- PROGRAM -

BAND CONCERT -- 2:30 P. M.
FAIRFIELD SCHOOL BAND
Directed by John Scott Francis
(Director, Earl Kinker)

3:00 P. M.
"THE STAR SPANGLED BANNER"

INVOCATION - Rev. C. L. Shook
Pastor, Valley Chapel Community Church

MASTER OF CEREMONIES
CUSTER B. REYNOLDS, Principal, Fairfield Hi

INTRODUCTIONS

DR. ARTHUR F. SCHALK
President, Fairfield Residents Associat

FAIRFIELD CITY OFFICIALS
CIVIC ORGANIZATION REPRESENTATIVES

ROBERT F. WESSEL, Mayor

DR. HOWARD WHITE
Chairman, Dept. of Government, Miami Iniver

CLARENCE SNYDER, Municipal Engineer

COLEMAN TRAINER, Contractor

JUDGE P. P. BOLI, Common Pleas Court

HONORABLE PAUL F. SCHENCK
Representative to Congres - Third Ohio Dis

ERWORKS OPENS OFFICIALLY

CITY BENEFITS ARE OUTLINED AT PROGRAM

500 Attend Dedication Of Plant, Groh & River Rd.

FACILITY

Erected At Total Cost Of $1,525,000 And Serves 1,400 Customers

By NONNY WILLIAMSON
Fairfield Correspondent
For the Journal-News

The dedication and formal opening of Fairfield's new $1,525,000 waterworks, sponsored by the Fairfield Residents Association, took place Sunday at the site on Groh Dr. and E. River Rd., with about 500 in attendance throughout the afternoon.

The program, Robert Swain, president of the Residents, in charge, was opened with invocation by the Rev. Hugo Mentink, assistant pastor of St. Ann Church.

Mayor Robert Wessel officially opened the valve, and commended all those who worked on the project for their foresight and industry. "This project is the first of many that are necessary for the growth of our city," he stated.

Unlimited Supply

Custer Reynolds, Fairfield High School principal, spoke briefly on the benefits of the waterworks for the city. "Our almost unlimited supply of water, which the Federal government says is one of the largest in the nation, could supply a dozen large industries," he said. "Fairfield's favorable location and accessibility, coupled with an abundance of gas, electricity and water, point to greater commercial, industrial and residential development."

Mr. Swain introduced city officials and employes, representatives of Fairfield clubs and guests who were seated on the platform.

The program closed with benediction by the Rev. Louis F. Ferry, pastor of Symmes Community Church.

Many of the visitors took advantage of the opportunity to tour the waterworks, and the hot weather made the drinking fountain, bearing a large sign "Fairfield's Fountain of Youth," quite an attraction. The helicopter was ...

MAYOR ROBERT WESSEL is shown formally opening the $1,525,000 Fairfield Waterworks during the dedication program held Sunday afternoon at the plant, Groh Dr. and E. River Rd. Pictured, left to right, are Jesse Juey, general chairman of program; Robert E. Swain, president of the Fairfield Residents Association and master of ceremonies of the program; Mayor Wessel, and Custer B. Reynolds, principal of Fairfield High School, who spoke.

Journal-News Staff Photo (Bart Kramer)

25 Persons Injured In 15 Weekend Traffic Accidents

Nine Of Victims Hurt In Two-Car Crash On Rte. 747; Three Motorists Are Cited

As vehicular traffic reached the season's peak in Hamilton and Butler County over the weekend, a total of 15 traffic accidents was reported by the Hamilton police, the sheriff's office, and the state highway patrol.

Twenty-five persons were injured, two seriously. Three motorists were cited in the City of Hamilton on traffic violation charges.

... in connection with accidents.

Nine were hurt at 5:45 p. m. Saturday at the intersection of Rte. 747 (Princeton Glendale Rd.) and Hamilton-Mason Rd. when automobiles driven by James S. Cress, 28, 1229 Pascal Ave., and Gregory Hostince, 44, 44 Ridgeway Dr., Cincinnati, collided.

Sgt. Clarence Blevins and Deputies Howard Cook and Ralph Kearney of the sheriff's department reported Cress was eastbound on Hamilton-Mason Rd. and Hostince southbound on Rte. 747.

Cross Serious

In serious condition at Mercy Hospital Monday morning are Cress, who suffered skull and arm fractures, and Mrs. Mary Sherman, 41, 43 Shadynook Dr., Cincinnati, a passenger in the Hostince automobile, who received spine and rib injuries.

Four Youths Held In Burglary Try

Sheriff's deputies arrested four youths at 1:30 a.m. Monday on charges of attempted breaking and entering during the night season after they were found parked in an automobile near Popp's ...

Hottest Days Are Recorded; More Of Same

Temperature Hits 95 On Sunday Afternoon For Season's High

BULLETIN

The official Hamilton temperature at 12 o'clock noon Monday was 94 degrees.

Saturday and Sunday were the two hottest days of the season and more hot and humid weather is forecast for the Hamilton area.

John Suedkamp, official weather observer for the Journal-News, reported the temperature climbed ...

Left to right — Mayor Robert Wessel, Ray Ross, Director of Region 2-A (Ohio) UAW-AFL-CIO; Leonard Woodcock, Vice-President, UAW who represented Walter P. Reuther, President who was ill and Adrian Jones, President of Local No. 233.

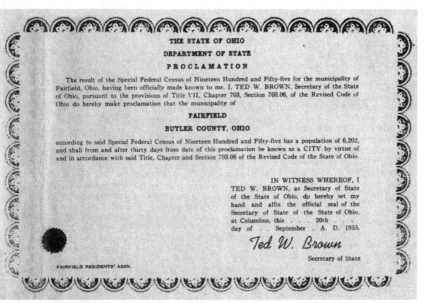

THE STATE OF OHIO

DEPARTMENT OF STATE

PROCLAMATION

The result of the Special Federal Census of Nineteen Hundred and Fifty-five for the municipality of Fairfield, Ohio, having been officially made known to me, I, TED W. BROWN, Secretary of the State of Ohio, pursuant to the provisions of Title VII, Chapter 703, Section 703.06, of the Revised Code of Ohio do hereby make proclamation that the municipality of

FAIRFIELD

BUTLER COUNTY, OHIO

according to said Special Federal Census of Nineteen Hundred and Fifty-five has a population of 6,202, and shall from and after thirty days from date of this proclamation be known as a CITY by virtue of and in accordance with said Title, Chapter and Section 703.06 of the Revised Code of the State of Ohio.

IN WITNESS WHEREOF, I TED W. BROWN, as Secretary of State of the State of Ohio, do hereby set my hand and affix the official seal of the Secretary of State of the State of Ohio, at Columbus, this . . . . 20th . . . . day of . . September . A. D. 1955.

Ted W. Brown

Secretary of State

FAIRFIELD RESIDENTS' ASSN.

FISHER BODY PLANT

OHIO ROUTE FOUR

ROLLING HILLS
SUBDIVISION

PLEASANT AVENUE

MARIE AVENUE

RIVER ROAD

EAST RIVER ROAD

HUSKINS ROAD

Fairfield, Ohio
circa 1955

MAYOR RECEIVES FAIRFIELD PROCLAMATION

Robert F. Wessel, left, mayor of Fairfield, Ohio, receives the certificate from Ted W. Brown, secretary of state, proclaiming Fairfield in Butler County, a city, at Columbus Tuesday. The proclamation is effective in 30 days. A special Federal census showed the village to have reached the 5000 population required to become a city.

Salute to Fairfield

Ohio's Newest City

FAIRFIELD SCHOOL DINING ROOM

THURSDAY, OCTOBER 20TH, 1955

Fairfield, Ohio

PRESENTED BY

THE FAIRFIELD RESIDENTS ASSOCIATION

DR. ARTHUR F. SCHALK, CHAIRMAN

Pioneer Of The Past - Avenue Of The Future

(Reprinted October 20, 1970)

Season's Greetings
1989

FAIRFIELD CHAMBER OF COMMERCE
& CITY OF FAIRFIELD

ORIGINAL
PROPERTY OF
ESTHER R.
BENZINO

FIRST FAIRFIELD CITY BUILDING

Fairfield Council Directs Growth Of New City

Pictured above are members of the first Fairfield City Council, a group of men and women completing their first terms as city officers, although many of them served when the area was a village. They have directed the sprawling promising city through its most difficult times and are most directly responsible for the great successes the city has enjoyed during its first two years.

Shown seated left to right are Treasurer Winifred Field, Clerk Walter Powell, President Larry Lloyd, Mayor Robert Wessel and Auditor Grace Hoelle. Standing, same order, Councilmen Francis Miller, Jack Daugherty, Solicitor Carl Kollstedt, Councilmen Ben Grob, Ellis Muskopf, Charles Vance, William Holden, Walter Hunter, and Public Service Director Paul Conrad.

0-595-22293-5

Made in the USA
Las Vegas, NV
16 December 2021

37992736R00083